THE PAMPERED CHEF®

Doris Christopher's

Main Dishes

Recipes at the Heart of Every Meal

Dear Friends,

Whether it's a busy meal during the workweek, or a special weekend gathering for family and friends, once you have the perfect main course, the rest of the meal just seems to fall into place. Our new cookbook, *Main Dishes, Recipes at the Heart of Every Meal*, was created to help you make main courses that truly put your heart into every meal.

Each recipe in this wonderful book will give you delicious and dramatic results. From the quick, easy recipes that are perfect for the weekday whirlwind, to cooking strategies such as Cook Once, Serve Twice, where an ingredient from a featured main recipe becomes the basis for a second sensational meal, *Main Dishes* offers mealtime solutions for every occasion.

In *Main Dishes*, we feature delectable color photographs of every delicious recipe, as well as preparation and cook times, nutritional information and special Kitchen Tips. So, from our Test Kitchens to your home kitchen, here's to making the heart of your meals a main event for your family and friends!

Warmly,

Doris Christopher

Doris Christopher
Founder and President
The Pampered Chef, Ltd.

Cover recipe: **Italian Sausage Charlotte** p. 119

The Pampered Chef is the premier direct-seller of high-quality kitchen tools sold through in-home Kitchen Shows presented by Kitchen Consultants across the U.S., Canada and the United Kingdom. At Kitchen Shows, guests enjoy product and recipe demonstrations, learn quick and easy food preparation techniques, and have lots of fun!

Founded in 1980 by educator and home economist Doris Christopher, and headquartered in Addison, Illinois, The Pampered Chef is committed to enhancing family life by providing quality kitchen products supported by superior service and information.

Contents

Weekday Express: *Main Dishes in 30 Minutes or Less*

*W*ith hectic schedules, getting dinner on the table Monday through Friday is a challenge. When there's not much time for cooking, turn to this chapter of easy, one-dish dinners and speedy skillet suppers. Our simple recipes for savory soups and sizzling sandwiches make satisfying weekday fare. Colorful, fresh stir-fries are ready in 30 minutes or less from start to finish. Using helpful cookware and tools from The Pampered Chef, you'll rediscover the joy of sharing home-cooked family meals every busy night of the week.

Family Investments: Cook Once, Serve Twice

*O*ur investment cooking strategy is guaranteed to save you time in the kitchen and add excitement to your dinner menus. We help you with the planning. First, there's a tasty recipe for tonight's dinner. The next night, planned-overs (not just leftovers) get served in a totally new, imaginative way. Make our corned beef dinner on Sunday, then whip up Reuben-style quesadillas on Monday, in less than 30 minutes. You'll find using a Stoneware Baker with a Lid/Bowl cover makes meats and poultry turn out so tender and juicy they can be enjoyed at two meals. Look for great ground beef ideas and grilled vegetable selections, too.

Portable Pleasures: *Perfect Foods for Patios, Picnics or Potlucks*

We all like to eat out – on the patio, in the park, at the potluck supper – and it's good home cooking that we like to eat most. So fire up the grill for Cajun-spiced beef sandwiches or sweet-sassy barbecued ribs. Cool down with summer salads – dilly pasta shrimp, curried chicken, tuna with marinated vegetables – while relaxing with your family on the patio. Picnic in the park with wrap sandwiches and round loaves stuffed with sandwich fixin's. Treat friends to the best potluck casseroles they've ever tasted. It's all possible with recipes from The Pampered Chef.

Gracious Gatherings: *Special Fare for Family & Friends*

Company's coming...the family's gathering. Celebrate with festive foods and warm conversation. Whether you're welcoming the day with a glorious brunch, hosting a backyard barbecue or planning a Sunday dinner, count on help from The Pampered Chef. Using high-quality kitchen tools makes preparing these exceptional recipes a pleasure. Come to the table with creamy seafood lasagna, stuffed pork chops or elegant beef pot pie baked in beautiful, hand-glazed Stoneware Bakers. Wake sleepy-eyed guests with omelet rolls or savory pastry braids baked to perfection on pieces of our classic Stoneware. Whatever the occasion, The Pampered Chef makes it special.

Weekday Express

Main Dishes in 30 Minutes or Less

Curly Pasta & Chicken Toss p. 6

Cook's Tips

▲ Spaghetti can be substituted for fusilli, if desired.

▲ One teaspoon dried basil leaves can be used in place of the fresh basil.

▲ It's important to use condensed chicken broth (a 10½-ounce can without any water added) to get the best chicken flavor in this pasta dish.

Tool Tip

▲ The **Stir-Fry Skillet** is a deep skillet with high sides that allows you to stir and toss ingredients for fast, even cooking. It works equally well on electric or gas stovetops, as well as ceramic cooktops.

Curly Pasta & Chicken Toss

Prep and cook time: 30 minutes

Fusilli pasta is long, spiral-shaped spaghetti. It adds a new twist to stir-fried chicken and vegetables.

1 package (8 ounces) uncooked fusilli pasta

2 tablespoons cornstarch

½ teaspoon salt

1 can (10½ ounces) condensed chicken broth

1 lemon

2 large carrots

1 medium red bell pepper

1 pound boneless, skinless chicken breast halves

2 teaspoons vegetable oil, divided

2 garlic cloves, pressed

2 cups broccoli flowerets

2 tablespoons fresh snipped basil leaves

1 ounce fresh Parmesan cheese, grated (about ¼ cup)

Menu Suggestion

Complete your meal with crisp sesame seed bread sticks and purchased angel food cake served with sliced fresh strawberries and fat-free frozen whipped topping.

1. Cook pasta according to package directions in **4-Qt. Casserole**. Drain and keep warm.

2. Meanwhile, combine cornstarch and salt in **Small Batter Bowl**. Whisk in chicken broth using **Mini-Whipper**; set aside. Zest lemon using **Lemon Zester/Scorer**; add to chicken broth mixture. Cut carrots diagonally into ¼-inch-thick slices using **Crinkle Cutter**. Cut bell pepper into 1-inch pieces using **Utility Knife**.

3. Cut chicken into 1-inch strips using **Chef's Knife**. Heat 1 teaspoon of the oil in **Stir-Fry Skillet** over medium-high heat until hot. Press garlic into skillet using **Garlic Press**. Add chicken; stir-fry 5 minutes, stirring with **Bamboo Spoon**. Remove from skillet. Heat remaining 1 teaspoon oil in skillet; add carrots and stir-fry 2 minutes. Add broccoli and bell pepper; stir-fry 2-3 minutes until vegetables are crisp-tender.

4. Add broth mixture and browned chicken. Bring to a boil; reduce heat to medium and cook until mixture is slightly thickened, stirring occasionally. Remove from heat. Stir in fusilli and basil. Serve immediately using **Nylon Slotted Server**. Grate Parmesan cheese over pasta using **Deluxe Cheese Grater**. Top with coarsely ground black pepper, if desired.

Yield: 4 servings

LIGHT Nutrients per serving: Calories 370, Fat 8 g, Sodium 950 mg, Dietary Fiber 3 g

Baked Potato Soup

Pictured on p. 8

Prep and cook time: 25 minutes

This chunky cream soup is a delicious encore for baked potatoes.

4 medium baked potatoes
2 slices bacon
1/2 cup celery, chopped
1/2 cup green onions with tops, thinly sliced
1 can (14 1/2 ounces) chicken broth
1 1/2 cups milk
1 garlic clove, pressed
1/2 teaspoon salt
1/4 teaspoon ground black pepper
1 cup light sour cream
2 ounces cheddar cheese, shredded (1/2 cup)

1. Remove skins from baked potatoes. In **Classic Batter Bowl**, coarsely mash potatoes with **Nylon Masher**.

2. In **4-Qt. Casserole**, cook bacon over medium heat until crisp. Remove bacon to paper towel to drain; crumble and set aside. Discard all but 1/2 teaspoon drippings in pan.

3. Meanwhile, chop celery with **Food Chopper**. Thinly slice green onions with **Utility Knife**. Add chicken broth, milk, mashed potatoes, celery, onions, garlic, salt and black pepper to drippings in pan. Bring to a boil. Reduce heat; simmer 10 minutes.

4. Stir in sour cream and reserved bacon. Ladle soup into 4 bowls using **Nylon Ladle**. Shred 2 tablespoons cheese over each serving using **Deluxe Cheese Grater**.

Yield: 4 servings

Nutrients per serving (1 3/4 cups): Calories 340, Fat 15 g, Sodium 970 mg, Dietary Fiber 2 g

Menu Suggestion

Serve this soup with a simple salad of sliced tomatoes drizzled with olive oil and red wine vinegar. Sprinkle tomatoes with chopped fresh parsley and green onions, if desired. Serve with crisp bread sticks or Melba toast.

Kitchen Tips

Tool Tip

▲ Fresh garlic adds a wonderful flavor to many recipes. Our **Garlic Press** is a real time-saving tool because you never need to peel the garlic cloves before pressing.

Make-Ahead Tip

▲ Make this recipe with planned-over baked potatoes. Just bake extra potatoes for a weekend meal and you'll be ready to make this soup on a weeknight. If you don't have leftover baked potatoes, scrub and prick potatoes with the **Hold 'N Slice™** then bake in 400°F oven 1 hour or microwave on HIGH 11-13 minutes until fork-tender. Cool slightly before using.

Crusty Grilled Sandwiches

Prep and cook time: 25 minutes

Hearty sandwiches are perfect fast-dinner fare. Our ham and cheese is grilled with a special garlic-Parmesan spread.

1 ounce fresh Parmesan cheese, grated (about 1/4 cup)

3 tablespoons butter or margarine, softened

1 garlic clove, pressed

8 slices sourdough bread

8 ounces sliced Monterey Jack cheese

8 ounces sliced deli ham

4 teaspoons Dijon mustard

1 medium tomato, sliced into 8 thin slices (optional)

4 teaspoons snipped fresh basil leaves (optional)

Menu Suggestion

Pair these grilled sandwiches with a mug of your favorite vegetable soup.

1. Using **Deluxe Cheese Grater**, grate Parmesan cheese into **Small Batter Bowl**. Add butter and garlic pressed with **Garlic Press**; mix well.

2. On 4 bread slices, evenly layer half of the Monterey Jack cheese and all of the ham.

3. For each sandwich, spread ham with 1 teaspoon mustard; top with 2 tomato slices and 1 teaspoon snipped basil, if desired. Cover with remaining cheese and bread slices.

4. Using **Large Spreader**, spread butter mixture over outsides of sandwiches. Place sandwiches on **Square Griddle**; cook over medium heat 4-5 minutes on each side or until golden brown, using **Nylon Turner** to carefully turn. Cut sandwiches in half with **Serrated Bread Knife**.

Yield: 4 sandwiches

Nutrients per serving (1 sandwich): Calories 530, Fat 33 g, Sodium 1760 mg, Dietary Fiber 2 g

Variation: **Southwest Crusty Grilled Sandwiches:** Use Monterey Jack cheese with jalapeño peppers. Substitute turkey for ham and fresh cilantro for basil. Prepare as recipe directs.

Cook's Tip

▲ Sourdough bread often comes in unsliced round loaves. For these sandwiches, just cut 8 slices, 1/2 inch thick, with the **Serrated Bread Knife**.

Tool Tips

▲ Use the **Ultimate Slice & Grate** with v-shaped blade to thinly slice the tomato.

▲ Remember not to leave your empty **Griddle** on a hot burner once you're through grilling the sandwiches. Doing so can discolor or damage it.

Baked Potato Soup p. 7, Crusty Grilled Sandwich

Rav'n Ravioli

Prep time: 15 minutes Cook time: 15 minutes

This saucy ravioli bakes along with the garlic bread in our Oval Baker. The tender, refrigerated pasta doesn't even need precooking.

1	medium green bell pepper
1/2	cup onion, chopped
1	teaspoon olive oil
1	garlic clove, pressed
1	jar (26-28 ounces) spaghetti sauce
2	packages (9 ounces each) refrigerated ravioli (any flavor)
1 1/4	cups water
12	French bread baguette slices (4 ounces)
1/4	cup butter or margarine, melted
4	ounces mozzarella cheese, shredded (1 cup)
1	ounce fresh Parmesan cheese, grated (about 1/4 cup)

Menu Suggestion

Complete your meal with buttered green beans or broccoli, fresh pear wedges and your favorite cookies.

1. Preheat oven to 400°F. Chop bell pepper and onion with **Food Chopper**. In **4-Qt. Casserole**, heat olive oil over medium-high heat; add bell pepper, onion and garlic pressed with **Garlic Press**. Cook 2-3 minutes or until vegetables are tender. Stir in spaghetti sauce, ravioli and water. Bring to a boil.

2. Meanwhile, use **Serrated Bread Knife** to cut French bread into 12 slices, 1/2 inch thick. Place butter in **Large Micro-Cooker®**; microwave on HIGH 1 minute or until melted. Add bread slices, tossing to coat evenly.

3. Using **Nylon Spoon**, spoon half of the ravioli mixture into **Oval Baker**. Top with mozzarella cheese, shredded with **Deluxe Cheese Grater**, and remaining ravioli mixture.

4. Arrange bread slices, slightly overlapping, around edge of Baker and pressed slightly into ravioli mixture. Grate Parmesan cheese over bread and ravioli mixture. Bake 15 minutes or until ravioli is heated through and bread is crisp and deep golden brown.

Yield: 6 servings

Nutrients per serving: Calories 630, Fat 31 g, Sodium 1340 mg, Dietary Fiber 5g

Kitchen Tips

Cook's Tips

▲ One package (25 ounces) frozen ravioli may be substituted for the refrigerated ravioli. Prepare as recipe directs.

▲ Very long, thin French bread loaves are called "baguettes." Slices from these thinner loaves can be arranged more easily around the edge of the **Oval Baker**.

Tool Tip

▲ Any extra grated cheese can be stored in the **The Grate Container™**.

▲ Risotto, an Italian specialty, is a deliciously creamy rice dish. Traditionally, risottos are prepared by gradually adding small amounts of liquid to Arborio rice as it is cooked and stirred until the liquid is absorbed. This cooking process is continued until the rice is creamy but still slightly firm.

▲ For a simple garnish, cut zested lemon into thin slices and place over chicken breasts.

Chicken & Asparagus Risotto Skillet

Prep and cook time: 30 minutes

Our 30-minute version of this creamy rice dish features instant rice, chicken and asparagus with a hint of fresh lemon.

6   boneless, skinless chicken breast
     halves (about 4 ounces each)
1/2 teaspoon salt, divided
1/8 teaspoon ground black pepper
1   teaspoon olive oil
1/3 cup onion, chopped
2   garlic cloves, pressed
2   ounces fresh Parmesan cheese,
     grated (about 1/2 cup)
1   lemon
2   cups milk
1   can (10 3/4 ounces) condensed
     cream of chicken soup
1/2 pound fresh asparagus spears, cut
     into 1 1/2-inch pieces (about 2 cups)
2   cups instant long-grain white rice

Menu Suggestion

Serve with crisp salad greens tossed with the *Italian Dressing* recipe found on our unique **Measure, Mix, & Pour™**. A frozen fruit-flavored Italian ice or sorbet makes a quick and refreshing dessert.

1. Season chicken breasts with 1/4 teaspoon of the salt and black pepper. Heat oil in **Large Skillet** over medium-high heat. Add chicken breasts; cook 5-7 minutes on each side or until chicken is no longer pink.

2. Meanwhile, chop onion using **Food Chopper**. Press garlic with **Garlic Press**. Grate Parmesan cheese using **Deluxe Cheese Grater**. Zest lemon with **Lemon Zester/Scorer** to measure 1 tablespoon zest.

3. Remove chicken from pan; keep warm. Add milk, soup, asparagus, onion, garlic, cheese, lemon zest and remaining 1/4 teaspoon salt to pan. Bring to a boil; reduce heat and simmer 3 minutes.

4. Stir in rice; top with chicken. Cover pan; remove from heat. Let stand 5 minutes.

Yield: 6 servings

LIGHT   Nutrients per serving: Calories 470, Fat 13 g, Sodium 820 mg, Dietary Fiber 2 g

Greek Turkey Burgers

Prep and cook time: 25 minutes

Tired of traditional burgers? This healthy sandwich has flavors reminiscent of Greek gyros.

1/4 cup plus 2 tablespoons onion, finely chopped, divided

1 pound lean (93%) ground turkey

1 container (8 ounces) nonfat plain yogurt, divided

1/4 cup seasoned dry bread crumbs

1 egg white

1 garlic clove, pressed

1 teaspoon dried oregano leaves, divided

1/2 teaspoon salt

1/8 teaspoon ground black pepper

2 medium tomatoes, sliced

2/3 cup cucumber, thinly sliced

6 pita bread rounds

6 lettuce leaves

Menu Suggestion

Serve these burgers with red grapes or marinated bean salad from the deli. Enjoy lime sherbet topped with fresh raspberries for dessert.

1. For burgers, finely chop onion using **Food Chopper**. In **Classic Batter Bowl**, combine ground turkey, 1/4 cup of the onion, 1/4 cup of the yogurt, bread crumbs, egg white, garlic, 3/4 teaspoon of the oregano, salt and black pepper; mix lightly but thoroughly using **Pastry Blender**.

2. For sauce, stir remaining 2 tablespoons onion and 1/4 teaspoon oregano into remaining yogurt; set aside.

3. Form turkey mixture into 6 oval patties, 1/2 inch thick. Using **Kitchen Spritzer**, lightly spray **Family Skillet** with olive oil; heat over medium heat until hot. Cook patties 10-12 minutes or until meat is no longer pink in center, turning once with **Nylon Turner**.

4. Meanwhile, use **Ultimate Slice & Grate** to slice tomatoes and cucumber. Cut one third off top of each pita bread to form a pocket. Fill each pita bread with lettuce, tomato, cucumber and turkey burger. Top with reserved yogurt sauce.

Yield: 6 sandwiches

LIGHT Nutrients per serving (1 sandwich): Calories 320, Fat 7 g, Sodium 660 mg, Dietary Fiber 2 g

▲ Partially freeze beef for easier slicing.

▲ Wash cutting board, knife and hands in hot soapy water after cutting raw beef and before cutting vegetables to avoid cross-contamination and prevent foodborne illness.

Make-Ahead Tip

▲ Cut beef the night before (do not marinate), wrap tightly and refrigerate. Vegetables can be cut also but wrap them separately from beef.

Spicy Beef & Broccoli Stir-Fry

Prep and cook time: 30 minutes

In a flash you can fix your family a stir-fry meal with bold, authentic taste. It's faster than carryout.

¼ cup light soy sauce
1 tablespoon cornstarch
2 tablespoons vegetable oil, divided
1 boneless beef top sirloin steak (1¼ pounds), trimmed
3 cups broccoli flowerets
1 medium onion
1 medium red bell pepper
2 garlic cloves, pressed
1 teaspoon peeled fresh ginger root, finely chopped
¼ teaspoon red pepper flakes
½ cup beef broth

Menu Suggestion

Serve over hot cooked rice or Asian noodles. Sprinkle with sliced green onions, snipped fresh cilantro or chopped peanuts, if desired. Serve with fortune cookies and hot tea.

1. In **Classic Batter Bowl**, whisk together soy sauce, cornstarch and 1 tablespoon of the oil with **Stainless Steel Whisk**. Cut steak lengthwise in half and then crosswise into ¼-inch-thick strips with **Chef's Knife**. Add beef to soy sauce mixture; toss to coat. Cover and refrigerate 15 minutes to marinate.

2. Meanwhile, cut broccoli into flowerets and onion into thin wedges. Cut bell pepper into thin strips, 2 inches long. Set vegetables aside. Press garlic with **Garlic Press**. Finely chop ginger root with **Food Chopper**.

3. Heat 1 teaspoon of the remaining oil in **Stir-Fry Skillet** over medium-high heat until hot. Add half each of beef, garlic, ginger and red pepper flakes to skillet. Using **Bamboo Spoon**, stir-fry 1-2 minutes or until outside surface of beef is no longer pink. (Do not overcook.) Remove from skillet; keep warm. Repeat with 1 teaspoon of the remaining oil and remaining beef, garlic, ginger and red pepper flakes. Remove from skillet.

4. Heat remaining 1 teaspoon oil in same skillet until hot. Add broccoli, onion and bell pepper; stir-fry 3-4 minutes or until vegetables are crisp-tender. Return beef to skillet; add broth. Bring to a boil. Boil 1 minute, stirring gently, until sauce is slightly thickened.

Yield: 4 servings

Nutrients per serving: Calories 400, Fat 18 g, Sodium 730 mg, Dietary Fiber 2 g

Cook's Tips

▲ Frankfurters, cut into 1/2-inch slices, can be substituted for the cubed ham.

▲ Any leftover soup should be covered and refrigerated. Soup will thicken once it is refrigerated, but when reheated in the microwave oven, the mixture becomes a saucy entrée.

Tool Tip

▲ Let your kids chop the broccoli and onion with our **Food Chopper**, just one of the many kid-friendly tools from The Pampered Chef. Kids of all ages like using the Food Chopper to chop candy-coated chocolate pieces, candy bars, hard candies and sandwich cookies for ice cream drinks and sundae toppings.

Mac 'n Cheese Soup

Prep and cook time: 30 minutes

By starting with a packaged macaroni & cheese dinner, you can have this soup ready in a jiffy.

1	package (14 ounces) deluxe-type macaroni & cheese dinner (including cheese sauce pouch)
1	cup broccoli, chopped
1/2	cup onion, chopped
1	cup water
2 1/2	cups milk
1	can (10 3/4 ounces) condensed cheddar cheese soup
1	cup cubed cooked ham

1. Cook macaroni according to package directions in **4-Qt. Casserole**; drain in large **Colander** and set aside.

2. Meanwhile, chop broccoli and onion using **Food Chopper**.

3. Combine broccoli, onion and water in Casserole. Bring to a boil; cook 2 minutes. Do not drain.

4. Stir in cooked macaroni, cheese sauce from pouch, milk, cheese soup and ham. Return to a boil, stirring occasionally. Ladle soup into 6 bowls using **Nylon Ladle**.

Yield: 6 servings

LIGHT Nutrients per serving (1 1/3 cups): Calories 380, Fat 14 g, Sodium 1438 mg, Dietary Fiber 3 g

Menu Suggestion

Make this meal with kid appeal. Serve with crisp carrot sticks made with our **Crinkle Cutter**. For dessert, cut apple wedges with the **Apple Wedger** and serve with a sweet dip made of 1 container (8 ounces) strawberry yogurt and 1/2 cup thawed frozen whipped topping.

Quick Chicken Cacciatore

Prep and cook time: 30 minutes

*This robust Italian dish, with tomatoes, mushrooms, onions and bell pepper,
uses convenient frozen chicken patties.*

1 package (10.5 ounces) frozen
   fat-free breaded chicken breast
   patties, partially thawed

1 medium green bell pepper

4 ounces mushrooms, sliced
   (about 1 cup)

1 small onion, chopped
   (about ¾ cup)

8 ounces uncooked linguine

2 cans (14½ ounces each)
   Italian-seasoned diced tomatoes,
   undrained

1 garlic clove, pressed
   Fresh grated Parmesan cheese
   (optional)

Menu Suggestion

Serve this one-dish meal with
refrigerated garlic bread sticks
baked on a flat **Baking Stone**. Add
a simple dessert of fresh green and
red grapes.

1. To partially thaw chicken patties, follow
   package microwave heating directions
   except microwave on HIGH 1 minute
   only. Cut chicken patties into ¾-inch
   strips and bell pepper into thin strips
   using **Chef's Knife**. Slice mushrooms with
   Egg Slicer Plus®. Chop onion using **Food
   Chopper**.

2. Cook linguine according to package
   directions in **4-Qt. Casserole**. Drain and
   keep warm.

3. Meanwhile, heat **Family Skillet** over
   medium-high heat until hot. Lightly spray
   with olive oil using **Kitchen Spritzer**. Add
   chicken patty strips; cook 5 minutes,
   turning frequently with **Nylon Turner**.

4. Add tomatoes, bell pepper, mushrooms,
   onion and garlic pressed with **Garlic
   Press**. Bring to a boil; cover. Reduce heat;
   simmer 8-10 minutes or until vegetables
   are tender. Serve over hot linguine.
   Sprinkle with Parmesan cheese, if desired.

Yield: 4 servings

LIGHT **Nutrients per serving:** Calories 230, Fat 1 g,
Sodium 1450 mg, Dietary Fiber 3 g

Kitchen Tips

Cook's Tips

▲ When cooking pasta,
always have the water
boiling rapidly before
adding the pasta. You
need to stir the pasta
only until the water
returns to a boil.

▲ Cacciatore in Italian
means "hunter." Some
say this style of dish
was developed by the
wife of an unlucky
hunter who returned
home with little more
than vegetables.

Tool Tip

▲ Grate fresh
Parmesan cheese with
the **Deluxe Cheese
Grater**.

Apple Oven Pancake

Prep and cook time: 30 minutes

*Breakfast for dinner? Absolutely! Give our puffy oven pancake
filled with cinnamon-spiced apples a try.*

1 cup milk

6 eggs

2 tablespoons butter or margarine, melted

1 teaspoon vanilla

1 cup all-purpose flour

½ teaspoon salt

2 packages (12 ounces each) frozen escalloped apples

1 tablespoon powdered sugar

1 teaspoon ground cinnamon

Menu Suggestion

Top this apple-filled pancake with vanilla yogurt or thawed frozen whipped topping for a special treat. Serve with hot cooked sausage links or patties.

1. Preheat oven to 450°F. Spray **Deep Dish Baker** with nonstick cooking spray. In **Classic Batter Bowl**, combine milk, eggs, butter and vanilla using **Stainless Steel Whisk**. Slowly whisk in combined flour and salt until egg mixture is smooth. Pour batter into Baker. Bake 10 minutes. *Reduce oven temperature to 350°F* and continue baking 15 minutes or until sides are crisp and golden brown.

2. Meanwhile, after 10 minutes of bake time, heat apples in microwave oven according to package directions. Remove pancake from oven. Fill center with apples.

3. Combine powdered sugar and cinnamon in **Flour/Sugar Shaker**. Sprinkle over pancake and apples. Cut into wedges using **Slice 'N Serve®**. Serve immediately.

Yield: 4 servings

Nutrients per serving: Calories 500, Fat 18 g, Sodium 530 mg, Dietary Fiber 4 g

Kitchen Tips

Cook's Tips

▲ As if by magic, this large pancake puffs like a huge popover while it bakes. When removed from the oven, it slowly sinks in the center making room for the apple filling.

▲ **Pantry Korintje Cinnamon** can be substituted for ground cinnamon.

Tool Tip

▲ Use the **Flour/Sugar Shaker** to sprinkle powdered sugar over cakes and brownies for a pretty, but low calorie, topping.

▲ Garnish cooked rice with fresh carrot zested with the **Lemon Zester/Scorer** and additional sliced green onions.

▲ Sesame oil, made from sesame seed, is a highly flavored oil. You only need a teaspoon to flavor this dish. It comes in both light and dark varieties, and either is fine to use here. Look for sesame oil in the grocery aisle with other oils or in the Asian food section of your supermarket.

Scrambled Egg Foo Yong

Prep and cook time: 30 minutes

In Chinese restaurants this dish is prepared pancake-style, but we've stirred up a simple egg scramble and added the traditional ingredients for Asian flavor and flair.

2	cups instant long-grain white rice
2½	cups water, divided
8	eggs
½	teaspoon salt
4	ounces mushrooms, sliced (about 1 cup)
⅓	cup green onions with tops, sliced
⅓	cup celery, coarsely chopped
1	cup fresh bean sprouts, rinsed and drained
1	teaspoon sesame oil
4	ounces uncooked medium fresh shrimp (⅔ cup), peeled and deveined
3	tablespoons stir-fry sauce or light soy sauce (optional)

Menu Suggestion

Complement this skillet dinner with a fresh spinach salad with mandarin oranges tossed with the *Asian Salad Dressing* recipe found on the **Measure, Mix, & Pour**™. Sprinkle salad with toasted sesame seed.

1. In **Large Micro-Cooker®**, combine rice and 2 cups of the water. Microwave according to package directions.

2. Meanwhile, in **Classic Batter Bowl**, beat eggs, remaining ½ cup water and salt with **Stainless Steel Whisk**; set aside. Slice mushrooms with **Egg Slicer Plus®**. Slice green onions using **Utility Knife**. Coarsely chop celery with **Food Chopper**.

3. Heat **Large Skillet** over medium-high heat. Add mushrooms, green onions, celery and bean sprouts. Drizzle with sesame oil. Cook vegetables 2 minutes, stirring with **Bamboo Spoon**. Add shrimp; continue cooking 2 minutes. Reduce heat to medium-low. Pour egg mixture over vegetables and shrimp. Cook, stirring occasionally, 6-7 minutes, until shrimp turn opaque and eggs are set. Serve with rice and stir-fry sauce, if desired.

Yield: 4 servings

LIGHT Nutrients per serving: Calories 390, Fat 13 g, Sodium 560 mg, Dietary Fiber 1 g

Tater-Topped Fish Bake

Prep time: 5 minutes Cook time: 25 minutes

On a busy day, this quick-to-fix fish dish will let you catch your breath while dinner is baking.

1 package (16 ounces) frozen broccoli, carrots and cauliflower vegetable blend

1 pound orange roughy fillets (about 4 fillets)

1 can (10¾ ounces) condensed cream of celery soup

1 package (8 ounces) shredded sharp cheddar cheese, divided

¼ cup milk

⅛ teaspoon ground black pepper

3 cups frozen shredded potato nuggets

Snipped fresh parsley

Menu Suggestion

Serve with whole wheat rolls and a quick fruit salad made of canned fruit cocktail, sliced bananas and miniature marshmallows.

1. Preheat oven to 425°F. Place vegetables in **Large Micro-Cooker®**. Microwave according to package directions. Drain well and lightly pat dry with paper towels.

2. Place vegetables in bottom of **Square Baker**. Top with fish fillets. In **Classic Batter Bowl**, combine soup, 1 cup of the cheese, milk and black pepper; mix well using **Stainless Steel Whisk**. Spoon over fish, spreading with **Classic Scraper**.

3. Top with potato nuggets. Bake 20 minutes; sprinkle with remaining 1 cup cheese. Bake 5 minutes or until cheese is melted and sauce is bubbly. Sprinkle with parsley.

Yield: 4 servings

Nutrients per serving: Calories 540, Fat 24 g, Sodium 1430 mg, Dietary Fiber 5 g

Kitchen Tips

Cook's Tip

▲ Kids are more apt to try a new recipe if something about it looks familiar. That's why we topped this dish with the crispy potato nuggets.

Tool Tip

▲ Use the **Kitchen Shears** to quickly snip fresh parsley and other herbs. Wash parsley and thoroughly dry, then cut off and discard stems. Place leaves in a small bowl and cut rapidly with tips of Kitchen Shears.

Chicken Tortilla Soup

Prep and cook time: 30 minutes

Make it light – make it Mexican! This soup proves low-cal, low-fat foods can still have loads of flavor.

4 (6-inch) corn tortillas
1/2 cup onion, chopped
3 boneless, skinless chicken breast halves (about 12 ounces)
1 garlic clove, pressed
1/4 teaspoon chili powder
1/4 teaspoon ground cumin
2 cans (14 1/2 ounces each) chicken broth
1 can (14 1/2 ounces) diced tomatoes, undrained
1 can (4 ounces) chopped green chilies, undrained
4 teaspoons fresh cilantro, snipped
2 ounces reduced-fat cheddar cheese, shredded (1/2 cup)
4 thick slices fresh lime (optional)

Menu Suggestion

Top each serving with a dollop of light sour cream. Serve soup with cornbread sticks and fresh oranges that have been cut into wedges.

1. Preheat oven to 400°F. Cut tortillas into 1/2-inch strips using **Kitchen Shears**. Place on flat **Baking Stone**. Bake 7-8 minutes or until crisp.

2. Meanwhile, chop onion using **Food Chopper**. Cut chicken into 1/2-inch pieces using **Chef's Knife**. Heat **4-Qt. Casserole** over medium-high heat. Spray with vegetable oil using **Kitchen Spritzer**. Add chicken; cook and stir 3 minutes. Add onion, garlic pressed with **Garlic Press**, chili powder and cumin. Cook and stir 2 minutes. Stir in broth, tomatoes and chilies. Bring to a boil. Reduce heat and simmer 10 minutes.

3. Snip cilantro using **Kitchen Shears**. Divide tortilla strips among 4 bowls. Ladle soup over tortillas using **Nylon Ladle**. Shred cheese over top with **Deluxe Cheese Grater**. Sprinkle soup with cilantro. Garnish each bowl with lime slice to squeeze juice into soup, if desired.

Yield: 4 servings

LIGHT Nutrients per serving (about 1 1/2 cups): Calories 290, Fat 9 g, Sodium 1320 mg, Dietary Fiber 2 g

Kitchen Tips

Cook's Tips

▲ Our **Pantry Southwestern Seasoning Mix** can be substituted for the chili powder and cumin. Use 1 1/2 teaspoons.

▲ This recipe can easily be doubled.

▲ Substitute reduced-fat baked tortilla chips for tortilla strips, if desired.

Tool Tip

▲ You'll save calories (and money) using the **Kitchen Spritzer**. Just fill the nonaerosol bottle with vegetable or olive oil, then lightly mist our nonstick **Cookware** before sautéing meats and vegetables.

Cook's Tips

▲ It may be necessary to cut string cheese sticks so they will fit end to end around the edge of the dough.

▲ We topped our stuffed crust pizza with a fast favorite, sliced pepperoni. But, you can easily use any pizza topping ingredients for this recipe. Family members may want to top different sections of the pizza with their own favorites.

Tool Tip

▲ If you have little chefs that love to cook, you'll like having **The Suds Pump™** at your kitchen sink. Liquid soap lasts 10 times longer, saving you money, and the hands helping with tonight's dinner will be squeaky clean.

Stuffed Crust Pizza

Prep time: 10 minutes Cook time: 18-20 minutes

You can make our version of this popular pizzeria pizza faster than you can get a pizza delivered – and you keep the tip!

Olive oil
1 tablespoon cornmeal
2 packages (10 ounces each) refrigerated pizza crust
1 package (12 ounces) mozzarella string cheese sticks (12 sticks), divided
1 garlic clove, pressed
1 can (8 ounces) pizza sauce
1½ ounces pepperoni slices (24 slices)
1 ounce fresh Parmesan cheese, grated (about ¼ cup)

Menu Suggestion

Serve this cheesy pizza with a salad of chopped romaine lettuce (use pre-washed and packaged greens), tomato wedges, garbanzo beans and pitted ripe olives tossed with Italian dressing. Grate fresh Parmesan cheese over top.

1. Preheat oven to 425°F. Using **Kitchen Spritzer**, lightly spray bottom of **Stoneware Bar Pan** with olive oil; sprinkle evenly with cornmeal. Unroll 1 package pizza dough across one end of Bar Pan. Repeat with remaining dough, filling pan. Press dough together in center with fingers to seal.

2. Place 10 of the string cheese sticks, end to end, around edge of pan on top of dough. Roll edge of dough over cheese making sure to keep covered cheese next to sides of pan; firmly pinch dough rolled over cheese to dough under cheese to tightly seal. Lightly spray surface of dough with olive oil.

3. Press garlic over dough using **Garlic Press**; spread evenly with **Skinny Scraper**. Spread pizza sauce over dough and slightly up sides. Top with pepperoni. Using **Deluxe Cheese Grater**, shred the remaining 2 string cheese sticks and Parmesan cheese evenly over filling. Bake 18-20 minutes or until crust is golden brown. Cut into squares.

Yield: 6 servings

Nutrients per serving: Calories 470, Fat 20 g, Sodium 1400 mg, Dietary Fiber 2 g

***Variations:* Italian Sausage Stuffed Crust Pizza:** Substitute ½ pound Italian sausage, cooked, drained and crumbled for the pepperoni.

Veggie Lover's Stuffed Crust Pizza: Substitute 1½ cups assorted fresh vegetables, such as mushroom slices, chopped onion or green bell pepper for the pepperoni.

Veggie Lover's Stuffed Crust Pizza

Farmstand Frittata

Prep and cook time: 30 minutes

You may want to visit the farmer's market to select the freshest produce for this colorful, open-face omelet.

6 ounces uncooked thin spaghetti
1/2 cup onion, chopped
1/2 cup red bell pepper, chopped
2 medium zucchini, sliced (1 1/2 cups)
2 tablespoons fresh basil leaves, snipped, divided
6 eggs
1/2 teaspoon plus 1/8 teaspoon salt, divided
1/4 teaspoon ground black pepper
1 1/2 ounces fresh Parmesan cheese, grated, divided (about 6 tablespoons)
1 teaspoon olive oil
1 garlic clove, pressed
3 plum tomatoes, seeded and chopped

Menu Suggestion

Round out your meal with warm dinner rolls and mixed fresh berries topped with a dollop of low-fat vanilla yogurt and a sprinkle of brown sugar.

1. Break thin spaghetti into 2- to 3-inch lengths. Cook according to package directions; drain.

2. Meanwhile, chop onion and bell pepper with **Food Chopper**. Slice zucchini with **Ultimate Slice & Grate**. Snip basil with **Kitchen Shears**.

3. In **Small Batter Bowl**, whisk together eggs, 1 tablespoon of the snipped basil, 1/2 teaspoon of the salt and black pepper using **Stainless Steel Whisk**. Add 4 tablespoons of the grated Parmesan cheese, grated with **Deluxe Cheese Grater**.

4. In **Large Skillet**, heat olive oil over medium-high heat. Add onion, bell pepper, zucchini and garlic pressed with **Garlic Press**. Cook and stir 2-3 minutes or until vegetables are tender; stir in cooked spaghetti. Reduce heat to low. Pour egg mixture over pasta mixture in pan. Cover; cook 14-15 minutes or until egg mixture is set in center.

5. Meanwhile, combine tomatoes with remaining 1 tablespoon snipped basil and 1/8 teaspoon salt. Grate remaining 2 tablespoons Parmesan cheese over frittata. Cut frittata into wedges using **Nylon Knife**. Serve topped with tomato mixture.

Yield: 6 servings

Nutrients per serving: Calories 230, Fat 8 g, Sodium 400 mg, Dietary Fiber 2 g

Kitchen Tips

Cook's Tip
▲ With the spaghetti added, our frittata has a firm texture, making it easy to slice and serve.

Make-Ahead Tip
▲ You can cook the thin spaghetti ahead of time and refrigerate, or use 3 cups leftover cooked thin spaghetti. Use the **Kitchen Shears** to cut leftover cooked spaghetti into 2- to 3-inch lengths.

Family Investments

Cook Once, Serve Twice

Caribbean Pork Roast p. 36, Paradise Pita Pockets p. 37

Cook's Tip

▲ Double the ground red pepper if you typically like your foods with a little more heat.

Tool Tips

▲ Use the **Pocket Thermometer** to check the temperature of the pork roast. The 10-minute standing time allows the internal temperature of the meat to rise to a safe eating temperature of 160°F or medium. At this temperature, pork will be juicy and have a slight hint of pink. If you prefer, cook pork to 165°F and let stand to rise to 170°F for well done.

▲ Use the **Hold 'N Slice™** to hold meat steady while slicing. It helps keep fingers away from sharp knife blades!

Caribbean Pork Roast

Prep time: 15 minutes Marinating time: 4 hours or overnight
Cook time: 1 hour, 30 minutes

Travel to the islands with a sweet-spicy pork roast, complete with pineapple, red onions and sweet potatoes. Tonight's roast is the start to tomorrow's pita sandwiches.

1	can (8 ounces) sliced pineapple, undrained
2	tablespoons packed brown sugar
2	teaspoons ground cumin
1	teaspoon ground cinnamon
1/2	teaspoon dried thyme leaves
1/8	teaspoon ground red pepper
3	garlic cloves, pressed
1	boneless rolled pork loin roast (about 3 pounds)
1 1/2	pounds peeled sweet potatoes (2-3 medium)
2	medium red onions
1/2	teaspoon salt
1/2	teaspoon ground black pepper

Menu Suggestion

Accompany this savory pork roast with a fresh spinach salad. For dessert, spoon cut-up fresh tropical fruits (or canned tropical fruit salad) over slices of pound cake. Top with pineapple sherbet and a sprinkling of toasted coconut.

1. Using small **Colander**, drain pineapple, reserving 1/2 cup juice for marinade. Combine reserved juice, brown sugar, cumin, cinnamon, thyme and red pepper in small **Colander Bowl**. Add garlic cloves pressed with **Garlic Press**.

2. Place roast and juice mixture in resealable plastic food storage bag. Refrigerate 4 hours or overnight to marinate.

3. Preheat oven to 350°F. Using **Crinkle Cutter**, cut sweet potatoes into 2-inch slices; cut slices into quarters. Cut each onion into 8 wedges and pineapple rings into quarters.

4. Remove roast from marinade and place in **Rectangular Baker**. Discard marinade. Place vegetables and pineapple around roast. Sprinkle roast, vegetables and pineapple with salt and black pepper. Cover with **Rectangular Lid/Bowl**. Bake 1 hour.

5. Using **Oven Mitts**, carefully remove Lid/Bowl, lifting away from you. Continue baking 15-30 minutes longer or until **Pocket Thermometer** registers 155°F for medium. Remove Baker from oven and let roast stand 10 minutes before carving. Cut about two thirds of roast into thin slices using **Chef's Knife**. Serve immediately with vegetables and pineapple. Wrap and refrigerate remaining roast for up to 4 days for use in *Paradise Pita Pockets (page 37)*.

Yield: 6 servings

LIGHT Nutrients per serving: Calories 370, Fat 6 g, Sodium 290 mg, Dietary Fiber 4 g

Paradise Pita Pockets

Prep time: 30 minutes

From planned-over Caribbean Pork Roast comes these fresh, colorful and healthy sandwiches – truly a taste of paradise.

Sandwiches

3/4-1	pound reserved *Caribbean Pork Roast (page 36)*
6	pita bread rounds
6	romaine lettuce leaves

Salsa

1	can (15 ounces) black beans, drained and rinsed
1	small red bell pepper, chopped
1	fresh mango, cut into 1/2-inch cubes (about 1 cup)
1/4	cup green onions with tops, sliced diagonally
2	tablespoons fresh cilantro, snipped
1/4	cup vegetable oil
1/4	cup white vinegar
3/4	teaspoon salt
1/2	teaspoon each ground cumin and granulated sugar
1/8	teaspoon each ground red pepper and cinnamon

1. For sandwiches, use **Chef's Knife** to cut pork roast into 1/4-inch slices; cut slices into strips about 1 inch wide and set aside.

2. For salsa, drain and rinse black beans using small **Colander**; place in small **Colander Bowl**. Chop red bell pepper. Cut mango into 1/2-inch cubes (see Cook's Tips). Diagonally slice green onions. Snip cilantro using **Kitchen Shears**. Add bell pepper, mango, green onions and cilantro to beans.

3. Combine oil, vinegar, salt, cumin, sugar, ground red pepper and cinnamon in **Classic Batter Bowl**; mix well with **Mini-Whipper**. Add bean mixture; mix lightly.

4. Add meat to Batter Bowl. Toss lightly with salsa. Cut pita bread rounds in half. Fill each pita pocket with lettuce and meat-salsa mixture.

Yield: 6 servings

LIGHT   Nutrients per serving (2 pita halves):
Calories 460, Fat 14 g, Sodium 920 mg,
Dietary Fiber 6 g

Menu Suggestion

Serve with sweet potato chips (or regular potato chips) and a sparkling fruit-flavored beverage.

Cook's Tips

▲ Purchase mango with unblemished yellow and red skin. It should yield slightly to pressure. If not, store in a paper bag at room temperature to ripen.

▲ To cut mango, stand it stem end up on a cutting board. Using **Utility Knife**, cut vertically on flatter side of mango from top to bottom about 1/2 inch to the right of the stem (alongside the large, flat seed). Repeat on opposite side. To make cubes, use tip of knife to score flesh, but not skin, in a crisscross pattern. Bend mango skin backwards so that cubes are raised above skin. Run knife under cubes.

▲ Save time by using jarred mango slices. They can be found in the refrigerated area of your grocer's produce section. Drain and cut into cubes.

▲ Substitute 1 cup cubed fresh peaches or nectarines for mango.

Cook's Tips

▲ Corned beef brisket is made by curing beef brisket in a brine. Cooking corned beef in our stoneware Lid/Bowl and Baker combination, results in moist, fork-tender meat.

▲ If corned beef comes packaged in liquid with seasonings, remove meat from liquid but do not rinse. Seasonings that adhere to the meat will flavor it during baking.

Tool Tip

▲ Use our handy **Kitchen Scale** to accurately weigh out the corned beef that needs to be saved for tomorrow's *Reuben Quesadillas*.

New England Corned Beef Dinner

Prep time: 15 minutes Cook time: 1 hour, 30 minutes

This complete meal slowly simmers in your oven. Plan to have enough leftover meat for our uniquely delicious Reuben Quesadillas (page 40).

Meat and Vegetables

1	corned beef brisket (3½ pounds)
4	cups water
1	bay leaf
2	garlic cloves, pressed
1	large onion
1	small head cabbage (about 1½ pounds)
4	medium carrots
3	medium, unpeeled red potatoes (about 1 pound)
⅛	teaspoon ground black pepper

Sauce

1	container (8 ounces) chive and onion soft cream cheese
¼	cup milk
3	tablespoons prepared horseradish

Menu Suggestion

Just add thick slices of crusty rye or pumpernickel bread to complete your meal.

1. Preheat oven to 425°F. For meat and vegetables, rinse brisket with cold running water; trim off excess fat. Pour water into **Rectangular Lid/Bowl**. Place brisket and bay leaf in Lid/Bowl. Using **Garlic Press**, press garlic over brisket.

2. Cut onion into thick wedges using **Chef's Knife**. Using **Crinkle Cutter**, cut cabbage into quarters and carrots into 2-inch lengths. Cut potatoes lengthwise into quarters. Arrange onion and cabbage around brisket. Top cabbage with carrots and potatoes. Sprinkle brisket and vegetables with black pepper. Cover Lid/Bowl with **Rectangular Baker**. Bake 1½ hours or until brisket is fork-tender. Carefully remove Baker from Lid/Bowl, lifting away from you. Remove brisket and vegetables from Lid/Bowl.

3. For sauce, combine cream cheese, milk and horseradish in **Petite Saucepan**. Whisk with **Nylon Spiral Whisk** over medium heat until warm.

4. Carve brisket diagonally across the grain into thin slices. Wrap and refrigerate 12 ounces (about half) of meat for up to 4 days for use in *Reuben Quesadillas (page 40)*. Serve remaining meat with vegetables and sauce.

Yield: 4 servings

Nutrients per serving: Calories 610, Fat 35 g, Sodium 1250 mg, Dietary Fiber 8 g

▲ Quesadillas can be prepared with purchased corned beef from the deli, if desired. Use 3/4 pound thinly sliced deli corned beef.

▲ You'll find packaged broccoli slaw in the refrigerated produce section of your supermarket. It is a mixture of shredded broccoli, carrots and red cabbage. Cabbage slaw is also good in these quesadillas.

Reuben Quesadillas

Prep and cook time: 25 minutes

Made with leftover corned beef, broccoli slaw and flour tortillas, we think you'll like our fresh approach to classic Reuben sandwiches.

12 ounces reserved sliced corned beef from *New England Corned Beef Dinner (page 38)*

 2 cups packaged broccoli slaw

1/4 cup Thousand Island salad dressing

12 (6-inch) flour tortillas

 3 cups (12 ounces) shredded Swiss cheese

Menu Suggestion

Serve with frozen steak fries baked on a flat **Baking Stone**, cooked baby carrots, sprinkled with **Pantry All-Purpose Dill Mix** and fresh fruit.

1. Chop corned beef using **Food Chopper**.

2. In **Small Batter Bowl**, mix together slaw and dressing using **Classic Scraper**.

3. To assemble quesadillas, place two tortillas on **Square Griddle**. Evenly layer each with 1/4 cup cheese, 1/3 cup corned beef, 1/3 cup slaw mixture and additional 1/4 cup cheese; top each with second tortilla. Place griddle over medium heat. Grill quesadillas until golden brown on both sides and cheese is melted, turning once with **Nylon Turner**. Repeat twice with remaining tortillas, cheese, meat and slaw mixture. Cut quesadillas into wedges to serve. Serve with additional Thousand Island dressing, if desired.

Yield: 6 servings

Nutrients per serving: Calories 570, Fat 34 g, Sodium 1230 mg, Dietary Fiber 1 g

Roast Chicken & Garlic

Prep time: 25 minutes Cook time: 1 hour, 30 minutes to 1 hour, 45 minutes

Roasted garlic is mild and sweet, and imparts a wonderful flavor to this chicken and sauce.
Reserve half of the roasted chicken for White Lightning Chicken Chili (page 45).

1   roasting chicken (5½-6½ pounds)
2   whole heads garlic, unpeeled
1   small bunch fresh parsley, divided
½   teaspoon salt
¼   teaspoon coarsely ground black pepper
¼   teaspoon paprika
1   medium carrot
1   stalk celery

1. Preheat oven to 400°F. Remove and discard giblets and neck from chicken. Rinse chicken with cold running water; pat dry with paper towels. Trim any excess fat from chicken.

2. Slice off top quarter of each garlic head to expose garlic cloves. Separate cloves and discard loose papery skin but do not peel cloves. Place 10 cloves in cavity of chicken. Using **Kitchen Shears**, snip enough parsley to equal 1 tablespoon; set aside. Place remaining parsley in cavity of chicken. Tie ends of legs together using cotton string. Rub outside of chicken with salt, black pepper and paprika.

3. Coarsely chop carrot and celery with **Chef's Knife**. Place in **Rectanglar Baker**. Place chicken over vegetables. Lift wing tips up toward neck then tuck under back. Sprinkle remaining garlic cloves around chicken. Place **Rectangular Lid/Bowl** over Baker.

4. Bake chicken 1 hour and 15 minutes. Using **Oven Mitts**, carefully remove Lid/Bowl from Baker, lifting away from you. Continue baking 15-30 minutes or until **Pocket Thermometer** registers 180°F in meaty part of thigh and juices run clear. Remove chicken to **Large Grooved Cutting Board**. Tent with foil and let stand 10 minutes before carving. Remove meat from half of chicken; wrap and refrigerate for up to 4 days for use in *White Lightning Chicken Chili (page 45)*.

5. Meanwhile, remove garlic cloves from Baker using **Nylon Spoon**. Wrap and refrigerate 6 cloves for later use in *White Lightning Chicken Chili*. Gently squeeze the flesh from skins of 6 additional cloves into **Petite Saucepan**; mash with **Nylon Masher**. Using small **Colander**, strain juices from Baker into small **Colander Bowl**; discard vegetables. Skim fat from juices and discard. Add remaining juices to mashed garlic in saucepan. Bring to a boil over medium heat. Stir in reserved 1 tablespoon chopped parsley. Carve remaining half of chicken into thin slices. Serve sauce with chicken.

Yield: 4 servings

Nutrients per serving: Calories 310, Fat 12 g, Sodium 610 mg, Dietary Fiber 2 g

Kitchen Tips

Cook's Tip

▲ Wrap and refrigerate any extra remaining roasted garlic cloves. Use garlic to spread on slices of warm French bread, mix in creamy salad dressings, toss with hot cooked pasta or add to mashed potatoes.

Tool Tips

▲ Grind black pepper with our convenient **Salt and Pepper Mill**.

▲ While the chicken is roasting, prepare the perfect comfort food side dish – homemade mashed potatoes. If you use the **Nylon Masher**, you can mash the cooked potatoes right in your **Saucepan** without scratching the nonstick coating.

White Lightning Chicken Chili

Prep time: 20 minutes Cook time: 30 minutes

This contemporary chili, made without tomatoes, gives planned-overs from our Roast Chicken & Garlic recipe a whole new look.

3 **cups reserved cooked chicken from** *Roast Chicken & Garlic (page 43)*, **shredded**

6 **reserved roasted garlic cloves from** *Roast Chicken & Garlic*

1 **cup onion, chopped**

1/3 **cup fresh jalapeño peppers, seeded and chopped**

3 **cans (15 ounces each) Great Northern beans, drained, rinsed and divided**

2 **teaspoons vegetable oil**

3 **cans (14 1/2 ounces each) chicken broth**

2 **tablespoons Pantry Southwestern Seasoning Mix**

1/4 **cup lime juice**

1 **tablespoon cornstarch**

1 **tablespoon cold water**

1/4 **cup fresh cilantro, snipped**

1. Chop onion and jalapeño peppers using **Food Chopper**.

2. Drain 1 can of beans using small **Colander**. Transfer to small **Colander Bowl**. Gently squeeze garlic from papery skins into beans in bowl; mash using **Nylon Masher**. Drain remaining 2 cans of beans and set aside.

3. Heat oil in **Dutch Oven** over medium heat. Add onion and jalapeño peppers; cook 4-5 minutes or until onion is tender. Add chicken, mashed bean-garlic mixture, whole beans, chicken broth, Seasoning Mix and lime juice. Bring to a boil; reduce heat and simmer 25 minutes.

4. Combine cornstarch and water, stirring until smooth. Add cornstarch mixture to chili and continue cooking 5 minutes, stirring constantly.

5. Snip cilantro with **Kitchen Shears**; stir into chili just before serving. Ladle chili into soup bowls using **Nylon Ladle**.

Yield: 8 servings

LIGHT **Nutrients per serving (1 1/4 cups): Calories 290, Fat 9 g, Sodium 1090 mg, Dietary Fiber 8 g**

Menu Suggestion

Top chili with reduced-fat shredded Monterey Jack cheese, light sour cream or chopped avocado. Serve with a fresh fruit salad of cut-up melon, pineapple chunks and pomegranate seeds, along with warm cornbread sticks.

Kitchen Tips

Cook's Tips

▲ Wear plastic gloves when working with fresh jalapeño peppers. Their seeds and membranes contain oils that will irritate your skin. Use the **Quikut Paring Knife** to cut peppers in half, then remove seeds and membranes.

▲ For chili with more heat, substitute 1/3 cup chopped canned hot nacho slices for the jalapeño peppers.

▲ Substitute 1 1/2 teaspoons ground cumin for Southwestern Seasoning Mix, if desired.

Tool Tip

▲ Use the **Hold 'N Slice™** to easily shred chicken. The strong, stainless steel prongs will separate cooked chicken meat into thin long strands.

Cook's Tips

▲ If using a charcoal grill, light charcoal briquettes and allow about 30 minutes for coals to reach a medium cooking temperature. The surface of the coals will be ash-covered. Coals should be spread in a single layer. If using a gas grill, consult the owner's manual for heating directions.

▲ For added flavor, marinate vegetables in dressing up to 1 hour before grilling.

▲ Regular mayonnaise can be substituted for light mayonnaise.

California Grilled Vegetable Sandwich

Prep time: 20 minutes Grill time: 16 minutes

Grilled vegetables, brushed with a rosemary vinaigrette, fill a crusty French bread loaf tonight then top angel hair pasta tomorrow.

4 large carrots (about 1 pound)
2 medium yellow squash
2 medium zucchini
2 medium red bell peppers
6 medium portobello mushrooms (about 6 ounces)
1 medium onion
1/2 cup balsamic vinegar
1/2 cup olive oil
2 tablespoons dried rosemary leaves, crushed
2 garlic cloves, pressed
1 cup light mayonnaise
1 loaf (1 pound) French bread (about 30 inches long)
12 slices (8 ounces) provolone cheese

1. Prepare grill for cooking at medium temperature. Cut carrots, yellow squash and zucchini into 3-inch lengths. Slice vegetables lengthwise using v-shaped blade of **Ultimate Slice & Grate**. Cut bell pepper into 1-inch-wide strips using **Utility Knife**. Cut mushrooms and onion into 1/2-inch slices. Divide vegetables in half between two large pieces of heavy-duty aluminum foil. Spread vegetables to form a single layer.

2. Mix vinegar, oil and rosemary in **Measure, Mix, & Pour™** until blended; set aside.

3. Press garlic into **Small Batter Bowl** using **Garlic Press**. Stir in mayonnaise; set aside. Cut bread in half crosswise and then lengthwise using **Serrated Bread Knife**.

4. Place one foil piece with vegetables on grid of grill. Brush vegetables with half of the vinegar dressing using **Pastry Brush**. Grill vegetables, uncovered, 12-16 minutes or until tender, turning halfway through grilling time with **Bar-B-Tongs**. Bring foil up around vegetables; remove from grill. Repeat with remaining vegetables and dressing. Place bread pieces, cut sides down, directly on grid of grill. Grill 30 seconds or until lightly browned. Spread half of the mayonnaise mixture on cut surfaces using **Large Spreader**; reserve remaining mayonnaise mixture.

5. To assemble sandwiches, arrange half of the cheese over bottom halves of bread. Cover with half of the vegetables, remaining cheese and bread tops. Cut each sandwich into thirds. Wrap and refrigerate remaining vegetables for use in *Angel Hair Pasta with Grilled Vegetables (page 49)*. Serve sandwiches with reserved mayonnaise mixture.

Yield: 6 servings

Nutrients per serving: Calories 600, Fat 36 g, Sodium 1160 mg, Dietary Fiber 4 g

Angel Hair Pasta with Grilled Vegetables

Prep and cook time: 25 minutes

A convenience Parmesan pasta dinner gets topped with sautéed chicken and planned-over grilled vegetables.

2 cups reserved cooked vegetables from *California Grilled Vegetable Sandwich (page 46)*

12 ounces boneless, skinless chicken breasts (about 3 breast halves)

1 teaspoon vegetable oil

¼ teaspoon salt

⅛ teaspoon ground black pepper

2 garlic cloves, pressed

1 package (5.1 ounces) angel hair pasta with Parmesan cheese sauce (plus ingredients to make pasta)

1 ounce fresh Parmesan cheese, grated (about ¼ cup)

Menu Suggestion

Serve with warm sourdough bread and fresh apple wedges.

1. Cut chicken crosswise into thin strips using **Utility Knife**. Heat oil in **Large Skillet**. Add chicken, salt, black pepper and garlic pressed with **Garlic Press**. Cook and stir over medium heat 5-7 minutes or until chicken is no longer pink. Stir in vegetables; heat through.

2. Meanwhile, prepare pasta with cheese sauce according to package directions in **Medium Saucepan**.

3. Arrange pasta on serving plate; top with chicken-vegetable mixture. Grate Parmesan cheese over top using **Deluxe Cheese Grater**. Serve with **Nylon Slotted Server**.

Yield: 4 servings

Nutrients per serving: Calories 580, Fat 30 g, Sodium 950 mg, Dietary Fiber 5 g

Kitchen Tips

Cook's Tip
▲ Omit chicken for a meatless main dish.

Tool Tip
▲ Grating fresh Parmesan cheese over pasta, pizza and salads is an easy way to add wonderful flavor to your cooking. Our **Deluxe Cheese Grater** is convenient to use in the kitchen or right at the table. It can be used to grate all hard and semi-firm cheeses, carrots, nuts and even chocolate.

▲ This meal has an added bonus. Not only will you have enough turkey meat for our *Home-Style Turkey Hash (page 53)*, but you'll have 2 cups of cubed turkey to freeze for later use in a casserole or skillet dinner.

▲ Acorn squash is a type of winter squash and is harvested in the fall. It has an acorn shape and ribbed, dark green skin, sometimes with patches of orange. The flesh is deep orange and has a sweet flavor.

Autumn Roast Turkey Breast

Prep time: 30 minutes Cook time: 1 hour, 30 minutes to 1 hour, 45 minutes

Baking poultry in the combination Stoneware Baker and Rectangular Lid/Bowl makes it extra moist.

1	bone-in turkey breast (5-6 pounds)
1/4	cup butter or margarine, melted, divided
1 1/2	teaspoons rubbed sage, divided
1/4	teaspoon salt
1/4	teaspoon ground black pepper
1	medium acorn squash (1 1/2 pounds)
3	medium Braeburn or Rome Beauty apples
1/2	medium red onion
6	pitted prunes (optional)
3	tablespoons packed brown sugar

Gravy

	Turkey drippings
1/2	teaspoon Worcestershire sauce
2	teaspoons cornstarch
1	tablespoon cold water
	Salt and ground black pepper to taste

1. Preheat oven to 400°F. Rinse turkey breast with cold water; pat dry. Trim excess fat using **Kitchen Shears**. Place turkey in **Rectangular Baker**. Combine 2 tablespoons of the melted butter, 1 teaspoon of the sage, salt and black pepper; brush over turkey using **Pastry Brush**.

2. Carefully pierce rind of squash in 4-5 places using **Chef's Knife**. Microwave squash on HIGH 1 minute. Trim off ends; cut lengthwise in half and remove seeds. Cut crosswise into 1-inch slices using **Crinkle Cutter**. Place in large **Colander Bowl**. Core apples with **The Corer™**. Cut each apple crosswise in half. Cut onion into thick wedges. Add apples, onion and prunes to bowl. Add combined remaining 2 tablespoons melted butter and 1/2 teaspoon sage; stir to coat using **Mix 'N Scraper®**. Add brown sugar; mix well.

3. Surround turkey with vegetables and fruit. Cover with **Rectangular Lid/Bowl**. Bake 1 hour. Using **Oven Mitts**, carefully remove Lid/Bowl from Baker, lifting away from you. Continue baking turkey, vegetables and fruit, uncovered, 30-45 minutes or until **Pocket Thermometer** registers 170°F in thickest part of turkey breast and juices run clear. Remove turkey; let stand 10 minutes before carving. Remove vegetables and fruit; keep warm.

4. For gravy, strain drippings; skim off fat and discard. Pour drippings (about 3/4 cup) into **Petite Saucepan**; add Worcestershire sauce. Mix cornstarch and water; stir into drippings using **Nylon Spiral Whisk**. Bring to a boil over medium heat. Boil 1 minute, stirring constantly. Season to taste.

5. Carve half of turkey into slices; serve with vegetables, fruit and gravy. Cut remaining turkey into cubes. Refrigerate 2 cups cubes for up to 4 days for use in *Home-Style Turkey Hash (page 53)*. Freeze remaining turkey cubes for up to 3 months for another use.

Yield: 6 servings

LIGHT   Nutrients per serving: Calories 340, Fat 10 g, Sodium 1930 mg, Dietary Fiber 7 g

Home-Style Turkey Hash

Prep and cook time: 30 minutes

On cold winter weekends, this skillet dish is ideal for a family brunch.

2 cups reserved cubed cooked turkey from *Autumn Roast Turkey Breast* (page 50)

4 slices bacon

3 cups frozen, seasoned, chunky-style hash brown potatoes

3/4 cup green or red bell pepper or combination of both, chopped

1/4 medium red onion, cut into thin wedges

Freshly ground black pepper to taste

1 cup prepared turkey gravy

Menu Suggestion

Serve *Home-Style Turkey Hash* with steamed fresh spinach or collard greens and wedges of fresh melon.

1. Cut bacon into 1-inch pieces using **Kitchen Shears**. Place in **Large Skillet**. Cook over medium heat until crisp, stirring occasionally. Remove pan from heat. Remove bacon to paper towels to drain. Pour bacon drippings into small bowl and set aside.

2. Return 2 teaspoons bacon drippings to pan. Add frozen potatoes, forming a single layer. Cook potatoes, without stirring, over medium heat 8-10 minutes or until potatoes are browned on one side.

3. Meanwhile, chop bell pepper using **Food Chopper**. Cut onion into thin wedges using **Chef's Knife**. Stir potatoes with **Nylon Turner**; continue cooking 3 minutes. Add bell pepper and onion; continue cooking 2-3 minutes, stirring frequently.

4. Stir in turkey and reserved bacon. Drizzle mixture with 1-2 teaspoons bacon drippings to moisten, if desired. Heat thoroughly. Season to taste with black pepper.

5. Heat gravy in **Petite Saucepan** over medium heat, stirring frequently. Serve with turkey hash.

Yield: 4 servings

Nutrients per serving: Calories 450, Fat 22 g, Sodium 1720 mg, Dietary Fiber 3 g

Cook's Tips

▲ Recipe can be doubled. Potatoes will cook up crispy and brown if cooked in a single layer, so use the **Family Skillet** when doubling ingredient amounts.

▲ Frozen, seasoned, chunky-style hash brown potatoes come packaged in 28-ounce bags. One-half bag equals 3 cups.

Swedish Meat Loaf Supper

Prep time: 20 minutes Cook time: 1 hour, 15 minutes to 1 hour, 20 minutes

Mom's meat loaf goes continental with ground beef and pork, mushrooms and allspice. Half is saved for open-faced sandwiches served later in the week.

Meat Loaf

- 1 can (4 ounces) mushrooms (pieces and stems), drained and finely chopped
- 1/2 cup onion, finely chopped
- 1/4 cup fresh parsley, snipped
- 1 cup fresh rye or white bread crumbs (about 2 slices bread)
- 2/3 cup milk
- 1 egg
- 1 1/4 teaspoons salt
- 1/4 teaspoon ground black pepper
- 1/4 teaspoon ground allspice or nutmeg
- 1 pound lean (90%) ground beef
- 1 pound lean ground pork

Noodles and Creamy Gravy

- 1 package (12 ounces) uncooked egg noodles
- 1 jar (12 ounces) mushroom or beef gravy
- 2 tablespoons milk
- 1/4 cup sour cream

Menu Suggestion

Serve with buttered peas, and carrots cut with the **Crinkle Cutter**. Add a touch of autumn with warm apple crisp.

1. Preheat oven to 350°F. For meat loaf, finely chop mushrooms and onion using **Food Chopper**. Transfer to **Classic Batter Bowl** using **Handy Scraper**. Snip parsley using **Kitchen Shears**. Add parsley, bread crumbs, milk, egg and seasonings to Batter Bowl; mix well.

2. Crumble ground beef and pork into Batter Bowl; mix lightly but thoroughly. Shape meat mixture into loaf in **Stoneware Loaf Pan**.

3. Bake 1 hour and 15 minutes to 1 hour and 20 minutes or until meat is no longer pink in center of loaf and internal temperature of meat loaf reaches 160°F using **Pocket Thermometer**. Remove meat loaf to serving plate; let stand 10 minutes.

4. Meanwhile, cook noodles in **4-Qt. Casserole** according to package directions; drain. For creamy gravy, heat gravy with milk in **Petite Saucepan** over medium heat, stirring occasionally with **Nylon Spiral Whisk**. Whisk in sour cream; remove from heat.

5. Cut meat loaf crosswise in half. Cut one half into 8 slices and serve with noodles and creamy gravy. Tightly wrap remaining half and refrigerate for up to 4 days for use in *Millennium Meat Loaf Sandwiches (page 57)*.

Yield: 4 servings

Nutrients per serving: Calories 550, Fat 29 g, Sodium 990 mg, Dietary Fiber 2 g

Millennium Meat Loaf Sandwiches

Prep time: 20 minutes

A comfort food from last century greets the new one with style.

½   loaf reserved *Swedish Meat Loaf* (*page 54*)
¼   cup mayonnaise
¼   cup sour cream
1   tablespoon Dijon mustard
1   teaspoon Pantry All-Purpose Dill Mix
½   medium cucumber, scored and sliced
2-3   slices red onion, rings separated
4   slices rye bread

Menu Suggestion

Serve these open-faced sandwiches with pickled beet slices and sweet gherkin pickles. Offer cinnamon-spiced chunky applesauce and gingersnap cookies for dessert.

1. Cut meat loaf crosswise into 8 thin slices. Mix mayonnaise, sour cream, mustard and Dill Mix in **Small Batter Bowl**; set aside.

2. Score cucumber lengthwise with **Lemon Zester/Scorer**. Slice cucumber and onion using v-shaped blade of **Ultimate Slice & Grate**. Separate onion slices into rings.

3. To assemble sandwiches, spread half of the mayonnaise mixture on one side of bread slices using **All-Purpose Spreader**. Top with meat loaf, onion, cucumber and spoonful of remaining mayonnaise mixture.

Yield: 4 sandwiches

Nutrients per serving (1 sandwich): Calories 590, Fat 38 g, Sodium 870 mg, Dietary Fiber 3 g

Kitchen Tips

Cook's Tip

▲ Dried dill weed can be substituted for the All-Purpose Dill Mix.

Tool Tip

▲ Use the **Lemon Zester/Scorer** for scoring citrus fruits before slicing to make the prettiest fruit garnishes ever. You'll find zested lemon, lime and orange rind adds a freshness to many dishes and baked goods, and is so easy to make with this handy tool.

▲ If not using *Make-Ahead Ground Beef*, prepare *Tamale Round-About* with 1 1/4 pounds lean (90%) ground beef. Cook beef in **Large Skillet** for 8-10 minutes or until no longer pink; drain. Sprinkle with seasonings and continue as recipe directs.

▲ Mild or hot salsa can be substituted for medium salsa.

▲ Sherbet with *Cinnamon Chips* would be a perfect dessert. To make *Cinnamon Chips*, lightly spray 4 (7-inch) flour tortillas with water using **Kitchen Spritzer**. Sprinkle with combined 1 tablespoon sugar and 1/2 teaspoon ground cinnamon. Cut each tortilla into 8 wedges using **Pizza Cutter**. Bake on flat **Baking Stone** at 400°F for 8-10 minutes. Cool completely.

Make-Ahead Ground Beef

Cook 3 pounds of ground beef in our large Family Skillet for three great recipes.

3 pounds lean (90%) ground beef

1. Place ground beef in **Family Skillet**. Cook over medium heat 14-16 minutes or until no longer pink, breaking beef into crumbles; drain.

2. Place 2 cups cooked beef in resealable plastic freezer bag for later use in *Shepherd's Pie (page 61)*. Place 1 2/3 cups beef in freezer bag for later use in *Taco Ring (page 63)*. Label bags and freeze for 2-3 months. Use remaining 2 1/2 cups beef for *Tamale Round-About*.

Tamale Round-About

Prep time: 40 minutes Cook time: 35-40 minutes

Traditional Mexican tamales inspired the creation of this festive dinner dish.

Filling
- 2 1/2 cups *Make-Ahead Ground Beef* or 1 1/4 pounds lean (90%) ground beef (see Cook's Tip)
- 1/2 teaspoon chili powder
- 1/2 teaspoon ground cumin
- 1/4 teaspoon salt
- 1 jar (16 ounces) thick and chunky medium salsa
- 1/4 cup red or green bell pepper or combination of both, chopped

Corn Bread
- 1 1/2 cups all-purpose flour
- 1 cup yellow cornmeal
- 1/4-1/3 cup sugar
- 1 tablespoon baking powder
- 1/2 teaspoon salt
- 1 1/4 cups milk
- 2 eggs
- 1/4 cup vegetable oil
- 4 ounces sharp cheddar cheese, shredded (1 cup)
- Sour cream (optional)

1. Preheat oven to 375°F. Generously spray **Stoneware Fluted Pan** with nonstick cooking spray. For filling, place ground beef in **Family Skillet**. Sprinkle with seasonings. Stir in salsa. Cook over medium-low heat 5 minutes.

2. Meanwhile, chop bell pepper using **Food Chopper**; sprinkle in bottom of pan.

3. For corn bread, combine flour, cornmeal, sugar, baking powder and salt in **Classic Batter Bowl**. Add milk, eggs and oil; stir with **Mix 'N Scraper®** just until dry ingredients are moistened. Stir in cheese shredded with **Deluxe Cheese Grater**.

4. Spread 1 1/2 cups batter evenly over peppers in pan using **Skinny Scraper**. Top with filling and remaining batter, spreading evenly.

5. Bake 35-40 minutes or until top is lightly browned. Loosen corn bread from edge and center of pan with knife. Invert onto serving plate. Slice into 16 wedges using **Slice 'N Serve®**. Serve with sour cream, if desired.

Yield: 8 servings

Nutrients per serving (2 wedges): Calories 570, Fat 32 g, Sodium 810 mg, Dietary Fiber 2 g

Shepherd's Pie

Prep time: 25 minutes Cook time: 25-30 minutes

*Use frozen cooked ground beef and vegetables, along with pantry staples,
and a hearty casserole is ready in no time.*

2 cups frozen *Make-Ahead Ground Beef (page 58)* or 1 pound lean (90%) ground beef (see Cook's Tip)

1/2 cup onion, chopped

1 teaspoon vegetable oil

1 garlic clove, pressed

1/2 teaspoon salt

1/2 teaspoon dried thyme leaves

1/4 teaspoon ground black pepper

2 cups frozen vegetable blend such as mixed vegetables or peas and carrots

1 jar (12 ounces) beef gravy

4 servings (about 2 cups) hot prepared instant mashed potatoes (plus ingredients to make potatoes)

2 ounces cheddar cheese, shredded (1/2 cup)

Menu Suggestion

This casserole needs only crisp bread sticks and fresh fruit for dessert to complete the menu.

1. Preheat oven to 375°F. Open seal of freezer bag containing ground beef 1 inch to vent. Place bag in microwave oven. Microwave on DEFROST (30% power) 5-7 minutes or until beef is thawed.

2. Chop onion using **Food Chopper**. Heat oil in **Large Skillet** over medium heat. Add onion and garlic pressed with **Garlic Press**. Cook and stir 2-3 minutes or until tender. Stir in ground beef and seasonings. Add vegetables and gravy to pan. Bring mixture to a boil; spoon into **Oval Baker**.

3. Prepare potatoes according to package microwave directions in **Large Micro-Cooker®**. Shred half of cheese over potatoes using **Deluxe Cheese Grater**; mix lightly. Spoon potatoes into **Easy Accent® Decorator** fitted with **Open Star Tip**. Pipe potatoes around edge of Baker over meat mixture.

4. Bake 25-30 minutes or until thoroughly heated. Remove Baker from oven. Shred remaining cheese over potatoes; let stand 5 minutes before serving.

Yield: 4 servings

Nutrients per serving: Calories 610, Fat 33 g, Sodium 1350 mg, Dietary Fiber 6 g

Kitchen Tips

Cook's Tip

▲ If not using *Make-Ahead Ground Beef*, prepare recipe with 1 pound lean (90%) ground beef. Omit oil. Cook ground beef with onion and garlic in frying pan 8-10 minutes or until beef is no longer pink; drain. Stir in seasonings and continue as recipe directs.

Tool Tip

▲ It's convenient to use the **Medium Scoop** to fill the **Easy Accent® Decorator** tube with mashed potatoes. The Easy Accent® Decorator comes with six different tips for decorating cakes and cookies with icing or pies and desserts with whipped topping. Use it to make fancy deviled eggs and party appetizers, too.

Make-Ahead Tip

▲ Cooked ground beef can be frozen for 2-3 months.

Taco Ring

Prep time: 30 minutes Cook time: 20-25 minutes

This meat-filled pastry ring has been a Pampered Chef favorite for years. Use the Make-Ahead Ground Beef (page 58) that's stored in the freezer.

1²/₃ cups frozen *Make-Ahead Ground Beef (page 58)* or ³/₄ pound lean (90%) ground beef (see Cook's Tip)

1 package (1-1.25 ounces) taco seasoning mix

1 cup (4 ounces) shredded cheddar cheese

2 tablespoons water

2 packages (8 ounces each) refrigerated crescent rolls

1 medium green bell pepper

1 cup salsa

3 cups lettuce, shredded

1 medium tomato

¹/₄ cup onion, chopped

¹/₂ cup pitted ripe olives

Sour cream (optional)

Menu Suggestion

Serve with a refreshing salad of mixed greens, orange and grapefruit segments, and poppy seed dressing.

1. Preheat oven to 375°F. Open seal of freezer bag containing ground beef 1 inch to vent. Place bag in microwave oven. Microwave on DEFROST (30% power) 5-6 minutes or until beef is thawed. In **Classic Batter Bowl**, combine beef, taco seasoning mix, cheese and water.

2. Unroll crescent dough; separate into triangles. Arrange triangles in a circle on **Classic Round Stone** with wide ends overlapping in center and points toward outside. (There should be a 5-inch diameter opening in center.) Using **Medium Scoop**, scoop meat mixture evenly onto widest end of each triangle. Bring points of triangles up over filling and tuck under wide ends of dough at center of ring. (Filling will not be completely covered.) Bake 20-25 minutes or until golden brown.

3. Using **V-Shaped Cutter**, cut off top of bell pepper. Discard top, membranes and seeds. Fill pepper with salsa. Shred lettuce and chop tomato using **Utility Knife**. Chop onion using **Food Chopper**. Slice olives using **Egg Slicer Plus®**. Place bell pepper in center of ring; arrange lettuce, tomato, onion and olives around pepper. Using **Easy Accent® Decorator**, garnish with sour cream, if desired. To serve, cut with **Slice 'N Serve®**.

Yield: 8 servings

Nutrients per serving: Calories 370, Fat 21 g, Sodium 1170 mg, Dietary Fiber 2 g

Kitchen Tips

Cook's Tip

▲ If not using *Make-Ahead Ground Beef*, prepare recipe with ³/₄ pound lean (90%) ground beef. Cook ground beef in **Large Skillet** over medium heat 7-9 minutes or until beef is no longer pink; drain. Remove pan from heat. Stir in taco seasoning mix, cheese and water. Continue as recipe directs.

Tool Tip

▲ The **V-Shaped Cutter** is a great tool for cutting bell peppers, melons, citrus fruits and tomatoes into two fluted halves. To make even, v-shaped cuts, place a rubber band around the outside of the vegetable or fruit about halfway from the top. Use the rubber band as a guide when cutting through the skin or rind.

Portable Pleasures

Perfect Foods for Patios, Picnics or Potlucks

Salade Niçoise p. 66, Chicken & Berry Salad p. 67

▲ To prepare hard-cooked eggs, place eggs in **Small Saucepan**. Fill with enough cold water to cover eggs. Bring to a full boil. Remove saucepan from heat and let stand, covered, 20 minutes. Place saucepan under cold running water to cool eggs. Refrigerate eggs until ready to use.

▲ Substitute prepared French salad dressing for *French Dressing* recipe on **Measure, Mix, & Pour™**, if desired.

Tool Tip

▲ Cover the **Chillzanne® Platter** with its dome lid then snap on the **Chillzanne® Platter Handle** and your *Salade Niçoise* is ready to go anywhere.

Salade Niçoise

Prep time: 45 minutes Marinating time: 1 hour

A beautifully composed platter of marinated vegetables, hard-cooked eggs and tuna creates this French classic.

French Dressing (see recipe on **Measure, Mix, & Pour™**)

3/4 **pound small red potatoes (about 4)**

5 **medium carrots**

1/2 **pound fresh green beans**

2 **cups cherry tomatoes**

5 **hard-cooked eggs**

2 **cans (6 ounces each) albacore tuna, drained and flaked**

1 **can (16 ounces) pitted ripe olives, drained (1 1/2 cups)**

1 **package (10 ounces) mixed salad greens**

Menu Suggestion

Serve this French salad with croissants or crusty French bread baguettes. Cool off with a pitcher of lemonade made in the **Quick-Stir® Pitcher**.

1. Prepare *French Dressing* according to recipe on **Measure, Mix, & Pour™**.

2. Cut potatoes into eighths using **Chef's Knife**. In **4-Qt. Casserole**, bring 2 inches of water to a boil over high heat. Reduce heat to medium. Place **Steamer Insert** in Casserole. Add potatoes; cover and steam 10 minutes.

3. Meanwhile, cut carrots into 2-inch pieces using **Crinkle Cutter**. Cut pieces lengthwise in half. Remove stem end from beans; discard. Using **Utility Knife**, cut beans into 2-inch pieces (about 2 cups). Add carrots and beans to potatoes in steamer; cover and steam 8-10 minutes or until all vegetables are crisp-tender. Rinse vegetables with cold water to cool; drain.

4. In **Classic Batter Bowl**, toss cooled vegetables with 1/2 cup of the dressing. Fill three sections of **Chillzanne® Platter** with **Divider** with vegetable mixture. Cut cherry tomatoes in half; toss with 1/4 cup of the remaining dressing. Spoon tomatoes into another section of Platter. Cover and refrigerate vegetables 1 hour to marinate. Refrigerate remaining dressing.

5. To assemble salad, peel and cut eggs into quarters. Arrange eggs, tuna and olives separately in remaining sections of Platter. Place salad greens in **Chillzanne® Bowl**. To serve, use **3-Way Tongs** to divide greens among dinner plates. Invite guests to choose toppings from Chillzanne® Platter. Serve with remaining dressing.

Yield: 8 servings

Nutrients per serving: Calories 420, Fat 28 g, Sodium 590 mg, Dietary Fiber 5 g

Chicken & Berry Salad

Prep time: 20 minutes

Main-dish salads make refreshing entrées for warm-weather entertaining.

Salad

- 1 head (3/4 pound) romaine lettuce, torn into pieces (6 cups)
- 2 cups shredded cooked chicken breast
- 1/2 pint fresh raspberries
- 1 cup sugar snap peas, cut in half diagonally
- 1/4 cup pecan halves, toasted
- 1/4 cup red onion, cut into very thin wedges

Citrus Vinaigrette

- 1/4 cup frozen orange juice concentrate, thawed
- 2 tablespoons vegetable oil
- 1 tablespoon white wine vinegar
- 1/2 teaspoon Dijon mustard

1. For salad, combine all salad ingredients in **Chillzanne® Bowl**; toss lightly with **3-Way Tongs**.

2. For citrus vinaigrette, combine all vinaigrette ingredients in **Measure, Mix, & Pour™**; mix well. Just before serving, toss salad with vinaigrette.

Yield: 4 servings

Nutrients per serving: Calories 320, Fat 17 g, Sodium 90 mg, Dietary Fiber 4 g

Menu Suggestion

Serve this special salad with a basket of warm miniature muffins baked in our **Deluxe Mini-Muffin Pan**.

▲ Baby back ribs are really pork loin back ribs that are shorter and smaller thus making them easier to hold when eating. Pork loin back ribs will work equally well in this recipe.

▲ If using a charcoal grill, light charcoal briquettes and allow about 30 minutes for coals to reach a medium cooking temperature. The surface of the coals will be ash-covered. Coals should be spread in a single layer. If using a gas grill, consult the owner's manual for heating directions.

▲ Lemon pepper seasoning salt can be substituted for Lemon Pepper Seasoning Mix.

Make-Ahead Tip

▲ Ribs can be baked up to 2 days before being grilled. Wrap tightly and refrigerate until grilling time. The sauce can be prepared at the same time. Refrigerate in covered container.

Kansas City BBQ Ribs

Prep time: 20 minutes Cook time: 1 hour Grill time: 10 minutes

Barbecue lovers are passionate about their ribs, so we've developed a recipe that is finger-licking good. Grill time is short because the ribs are oven-braised first.

Ribs

4¹/2-5	pounds pork baby back ribs (2 slabs)
4	garlic cloves, pressed
1¹/2	teaspoons Pantry Lemon Pepper Seasoning Mix
3	cups tomato juice

Sauce

1¹/2	cups ketchup
1	cup packed brown sugar
¹/2	cup cider vinegar
¹/4	cup Worcestershire sauce
1	teaspoon chili powder

Menu Suggestion

Serve ribs with deli coleslaw, corn on the cob, watermelon wedges and frosted brownies for a sizzling summer meal.

1. Preheat oven to 400°F. For ribs, cut each slab into thirds using **Kitchen Shears** and place in **Rectangular Lid/Bowl**. Press garlic over meaty sides of ribs using **Garlic Press**; spread with **Skinny Scraper**. Sprinkle with Seasoning Mix. Carefully pour tomato juice around ribs; cover with **Rectangular Baker**. Bake 1 hour. Carefully remove Baker from Lid/Bowl. Remove ribs from Lid/Bowl. Discard tomato juice.

2. Meanwhile, for sauce, whisk together all ingredients in **Petite Saucepan** using **Nylon Spiral Whisk**. Bring to a boil over medium-high heat; reduce heat to medium-low and cook 10 minutes, stirring occasionally. Reserve ³/4 cup sauce for serving with grilled ribs.

3. Prepare grill for cooking at medium temperature. Place ribs, meaty side up, on lightly greased grid of grill. Brush with half of remaining sauce using **Pastry Brush**. Cover; grill 5 minutes. Turn ribs over using **Bar-B-Tongs**; brush with remaining sauce. Continue grilling, covered, 5 minutes. Reheat reserved sauce and serve with ribs.

Yield: 6 servings

Nutrients per serving: Calories 440, Fat 32 g, Sodium 1090 mg, Dietary Fiber 1 g

Italian Muffuletta

Prep time: 1 hour, 10 minutes Cook time: 15-20 minutes

This New Orleans classic has the usual meats and cheeses, and the bread is always round.
But the key ingredient – olive salad – makes the difference.

Bread

Olive oil
- 1 package (16 ounces) hot roll mix (including yeast packet)
- 1 cup hot water (120°-130°F)
- 2 tablespoons butter or margarine, softened
- 1 egg
- 1 garlic clove, pressed
- 3 tablespoons fresh Parmesan cheese, grated

Olive Salad

- 2/3 cup pimento-stuffed green olives, chopped
- 2/3 cup pitted ripe olives, chopped
- 2/3 cup celery, chopped
- 2 garlic cloves, pressed
- 1/2 cup Italian salad dressing

Sandwich Fillings

- 8 ounces thinly sliced deli meat such as hard salami, turkey or ham
- 4 ounces thinly sliced cheese such as provolone, Swiss or mozzarella

Menu Suggestion

Serve with potato salad from the deli and crunchy carrot and celery sticks.

1. For bread, spray **Deep Dish Baker** with olive oil using **Kitchen Spritzer**. In **Classic Batter Bowl**, combine hot roll mix and yeast. Using **Mix 'N Scraper®**, stir in hot water, butter and egg until dough pulls away from side of bowl. Turn dough out onto lightly floured surface. Knead dough 5 minutes until smooth. Cover dough with Batter Bowl; let rest 5 minutes. Using lightly floured **Dough and Pizza Roller**, evenly roll out dough in Baker. Cover loosely with plastic wrap and cloth towel. Let rise in a warm place (80°- 85°F) for 30 minutes.

2. Preheat oven to 375°F. Uncover dough and lightly spray with olive oil. Press 1 garlic clove over dough using **Garlic Press**; spread evenly with **Skinny Scraper**. Using **Deluxe Cheese Grater**, grate Parmesan cheese over dough. Bake 15-20 minutes or until deep golden brown. Remove bread from Baker to **Nonstick Cooling Rack**. Cool 10 minutes.

3. Meanwhile, for olive salad, chop olives and celery using **Food Chopper**; place in **Small Batter Bowl**. Add pressed garlic and dressing; mix well.

4. To assemble sandwich, cut bread in half horizontally using **Serrated Bread Knife**. Spread 1 cup of the olive salad over bottom half of bread. Cover with overlapping slices of meat and cheese; top with remaining olive salad. Cover with top half of bread. Cut into wedges.

Yield: 8 servings

Nutrients per serving: Calories 450, Fat 22 g, Sodium 1750 mg, Dietary Fiber 4 g

Kitchen Tips

Cook's Tip
▲ This sandwich is also delicious served warm. Place assembled sandwich on flat **Baking Stone**; cover loosely with aluminum foil and bake at 350°F for 20 minutes or until heated through.

Tool Tip
▲ Use the **Pocket Thermometer** to accurately check the temperature of the water when making the bread dough.

Make-Ahead Tip
▲ Bread can be made a day in advance. Cool completely; wrap tightly and store at room temperature. When ready to assemble, cut and fill loaf as recipe directs.

▲ These wraps make tasty party snacks that are low in calories and fat. Wrap filled tortillas individually with plastic wrap. Refrigerate, seam side down, for 30 minutes. To serve, cut each wrap crosswise into 6 slices to make 3 dozen party snacks. Serve on lettuce-lined **Chillzanne® Platter.**

Make-Ahead Tip

▲ Wraps can be prepared in advance. Wrap filled tortillas individually in plastic wrap and refrigerate up to 3 hours before cutting and serving as sandwiches or party snacks.

Thai Tuna Wraps

Prep time: 25 minutes

East meets West in these innovative tortilla wraps with a flavorful filling of tuna, crisp vegetables and Thai dressing.

2	tablespoons lime juice
1/2	cup fat-free mayonnaise, divided
1	tablespoon soy sauce
1	tablespoon sugar
3	cups cabbage, chopped
1	medium carrot, shredded
3	green onions with tops, thinly sliced
2	tablespoons fresh cilantro, snipped
1	can (6 ounces) water-packed tuna, drained and flaked
1	medium red bell pepper
6	(8-inch) fat-free flour tortillas
12-18	large, fresh spinach leaves

Menu Suggestion

Serve these wraps with a mixed fresh fruit salad and iced tea. A lemon dessert–sherbet, pie or bars–would be delightful.

1. In **Classic Batter Bowl**, whisk together lime juice, 2 tablespoons of the mayonnaise, soy sauce and sugar using **Stainless Steel Whisk**.

2. Chop cabbage with **Food Chopper**. Shred carrot using **Deluxe Cheese Grater** fitted with coarse shredding drum. Slice green onions using **Utility Knife**. Snip cilantro with **Kitchen Shears**.

3. Add cabbage, carrot, green onions, cilantro and tuna to soy sauce mixture; mix lightly. Cut bell pepper into 24 thin strips.

4. For each wrap, spread tortilla with 1 tablespoon of the remaining mayonnaise using **Skinny Scraper**. Top evenly with 1/2 cup of the tuna mixture. Cover with 2 or 3 spinach leaves and 4 bell pepper strips. Roll up tortilla tightly. Repeat with remaining tortillas and filling. To serve, cut each roll in half diagonally with **Serrated Bread Knife**. Serve using **Bamboo Tongs**.

Yield: 6 sandwiches

LIGHT Nutrients per serving (1 sandwich): Calories 190, Fat less than 1 g, Sodium 490 mg, Dietary Fiber 3 g

Cajun Grilled Beef Sandwiches

Prep time: 15 minutes Grill time: 17-21 minutes

Cool and creamy Cajun slaw tops tender strips of seasoned grilled beef to create one sensational sandwich.

1/2 cup mayonnaise
1 tablespoon finely chopped onion
1 tablespoon white vinegar
5 teaspoons Pantry Cajun Herb Seasoning Mix, divided
1/2 teaspoon sugar
5 cups packaged cabbage slaw mix
1 1/4 pounds boneless beef top sirloin steak, cut 1 inch thick
 Vegetable oil
4 kaiser bread rolls, split and toasted
8 thin green bell pepper slices (optional)

Menu Suggestion

Grilled pineapple slices and fresh corn relish are perfect accompaniments to this spicy sandwich.

1. Prepare grill for cooking at medium temperature. In **Classic Batter Bowl**, combine mayonnaise, onion, vinegar, 2 teaspoons of the Seasoning Mix and sugar; mix until well blended. Add cabbage slaw mix; mix lightly and set aside.

2. Lightly brush surface of steak with vegetable oil using **Pastry Brush**. Sprinkle remaining 3 teaspoons Seasoning Mix evenly over both sides of steak. Place steak on grid of grill.

3. Grill steak, uncovered, 17-21 minutes or until steak is medium rare (145°F) to medium (160°F) doneness, turning occasionally with **Bar-B-Boss**. Carve steak crosswise into thin slices using **Chef's Knife**.

4. For each sandwich, arrange one fourth of the beef slices on bottom of roll; top with 1/2 cup cabbage mixture and 2 bell pepper slices, if desired. Cover with top half of roll.

Yield: 4 sandwiches

Nutrients per serving (1 sandwich): Calories 660, Fat 34 g, Sodium 880 mg, Dietary Fiber 3 g

Kitchen Tips

Cook's Tips

▲ For tips on preparing your grill for cooking, see page 68.

▲ To broil steak, place on rack of broiler pan so that the surface of the steak is 3-4 inches from heat source. Broil 9-12 minutes for medium rare to medium doneness, turning once.

Tool Tip

▲ Use the instant-read **Pocket Thermometer** to accurately check the doneness of your steak.

▲ Use light mayonnaise and light sour cream and you'll save 75 calories and 9 grams of fat per serving.

▲ Substitute 2 teaspoons dried dill weed for All-Purpose Dill Mix, if desired.

▲ Chopped imitation crabmeat can be substituted for the cooked shrimp.

Tool Tip

▲ The **Chillzanne® Bowl** has a unique food-safe gel within the bowl's sides that, once frozen, will keep food chilled for hours. It's the perfect container for serving refreshing summer salads indoors or alfresco. Take leftover salad for lunch the next day in the **Chillzanne® Mini-Bowl.**

Make-Ahead Tip

▲ Salad can be made the day before serving. Cover tightly and refrigerate.

Dilly Seafood Pasta Salad

Prep time: 25 minutes Chill time: 30 minutes to overnight

Pack this chilled salad, featuring shrimp and pasta shells, for your next picnic at the beach.

Dressing

- 1 lemon
- 1/2 cup mayonnaise
- 1/2 cup sour cream
- 1 tablespoon Pantry All-Purpose Dill Mix

Salad

- 2 cups (5 ounces) uncooked medium shell pasta
- 1 cup cucumber, scored and sliced
- 1/2 cup red bell pepper, chopped
- 1/2 cup carrot, coarsely chopped
- 1/4 cup green onions with tops, thinly sliced
- 1/2 pound (8 ounces) shelled, deveined cooked medium shrimp
- 1/4 teaspoon salt

Menu Suggestion

Complement this salad with crisp sesame bread sticks and iced tea with lemon slices.

1. For dressing, zest whole lemon using **Lemon Zester/Scorer**. Juice lemon using **Lemon Aid** to measure 1 tablespoon juice. Combine zest, juice, mayonnaise, sour cream and Dill Mix in **Small Batter Bowl**; mix well.

2. For salad, cook pasta according to package directions in **4-Qt. Casserole**; drain and rinse with cold water. Using Lemon Zester/Scorer, score down length of cucumber in evenly spaced rows around entire cucumber. Slice cucumber using **Ultimate Slice & Grate**. Chop bell pepper and carrot using **Food Chopper**. Slice green onions using **Chef's Knife**.

3. Place all salad ingredients in **Chillzanne® Bowl**. Pour dressing over salad; toss lightly using **3-Way Tongs**. Cover; refrigerate at least 30 minutes or overnight.

Yield: 6 servings

Nutrients per serving: Calories 275, Fat 20 g, Sodium 400 mg, Dietary Fiber 1 g

Chicken Caesar Salad Wraps

Prep and cook time: 30 minutes

A popular salad gets wrapped in flour tortillas to create unique sandwiches.

2 boneless, skinless chicken breast halves (about 12 ounces)

Olive oil

2 garlic cloves, pressed

1/4 cup red onion, chopped

1/4 cup pitted kalamata or ripe olives, chopped

1/4 cup red bell pepper, chopped

1 ounce fresh Parmesan cheese, grated (about 1/4 cup)

4 cups romaine lettuce, thinly sliced

3/4 cup seasoned croutons

1/2 cup fat-free Caesar salad dressing

6 (8-inch) fat-free flour tortillas

Menu Suggestion

Arrange a colorful array of fresh vegetables and relishes on our **Chillzanne® Platter** to complement these light sandwich wraps. Add refreshing watermelon wedges, cut with the **Crinkle Cutter.**

1. Lightly spray chicken with oil using **Kitchen Spritzer**. Press garlic with **Garlic Press**; firmly press garlic into chicken using **Skinny Scraper**. Heat **Small Sauté Pan** over medium heat until hot. Cook chicken 15-20 minutes or until no longer pink in center, turning once with **Nylon Tongs**. Remove chicken from pan; cool. Slice into 1/4-inch-thick strips using **Utility Knife**. Place chicken in **Classic Batter Bowl**.

2. Chop onion and olives using **Food Chopper**. Chop bell pepper with Utility Knife. Grate Parmesan cheese using **Deluxe Cheese Grater**. Slice lettuce. Add onion, olives, bell pepper, cheese, lettuce, croutons and dressing to chicken in Batter Bowl; toss mixture to coat evenly with dressing.

3. For each wrap, place about 3/4 cup of the chicken mixture on tortilla. Roll up tortilla tightly. Repeat with remaining tortillas and filling. To serve, cut each roll in half diagonally with **Serrated Bread Knife**.

Yield: 6 sandwiches

LIGHT Nutrients per serving (1 sandwich):
Calories 270, Fat 5 g, Sodium 460 mg,
Dietary Fiber 5 g

Kitchen Tips

Cook's Tip

▲ These wraps make delicious appetizers. Wrap filled tortillas individually with plastic wrap. Refrigerate, seam side down, for 30 minutes. To serve, cut each wrap crosswise into 6 slices to make 3 dozen appetizers. Serve on lettuce-lined **Chillzanne® Platter**.

Tool Tip

▲ After chopping and slicing fresh vegetables and lettuce, use the **Handy Scraper** to easily transfer ingredients from the cutting board to the Batter Bowl.

Make-Ahead Tip

▲ Wraps can be prepared in advance. Wrap filled tortillas individually in plastic wrap and refrigerate up to 3 hours before cutting and serving as sandwiches or appetizers.

Greek Island Fish Packets

Prep time: 20 minutes Grill time: 18-22 minutes

Foil-packet grilling is the no-fuss way to cook. It may even bring back fond memories of summer camping.

1 medium onion, sliced

1 large green bell pepper, sliced

1 large zucchini, sliced (about 2 cups)

1 garlic clove, pressed

1 can (14½ ounces) Italian-seasoned diced tomatoes, undrained

4 firm, white fish fillets (about 4 ounces each) such as red snapper, tilapia or whitefish

Olive oil

¼ teaspoon salt

⅛ teaspoon ground black pepper

12 pimento-stuffed green olives, sliced

Menu Suggestion

Complement this flavorful fish with cooked couscous, a tiny granulated pasta. Plain or flavored, packaged couscous can be found in the rice or pasta section of your supermarket.

1. Prepare grill for cooking at medium temperature. Slice onion, bell pepper and zucchini using v-shaped blade of **Ultimate Slice & Grate**. Press garlic into **Small Batter Bowl** using **Garlic Press**; stir in tomatoes.

2. Cut four 18 x 12-inch pieces of heavy-duty aluminum foil. Place one fourth of the onion, bell pepper and zucchini slices in center of each piece of foil. Spoon ¼ cup tomato mixture over vegetables; top with 1 fish fillet. Spray fish fillets with olive oil using **Kitchen Spritzer**. Sprinkle with salt and black pepper.

3. Top each fish fillet with 1 tablespoon of the remaining tomato mixture and 3 olives sliced with **Egg Slicer Plus®**. Fold foil over fish and vegetables; double fold edges to seal, leaving room for steam inside each packet.

4. Place packets on grid of grill. Grill 18-22 minutes or until fish flakes easily with fork. Remove packets from grill using **Bar-B-Tongs**. Open packets carefully to allow steam to escape.

Yield: 4 servings

LIGHT Nutrients per serving: Calories 170, Fat 3 g, Sodium 1000 mg, Dietary Fiber 2 g

Kitchen Tips

Cook's Tips

▲ Our **Large Grooved Cutting Board** is the same size as the foil pieces needed for these packets. While using it for food preparation, it becomes a quick guide for measuring your foil pieces. If using standard-weight aluminum foil, use two sheets of foil for each packet.

▲ For tips on preparing your grill for cooking, see page 68.

Make-Ahead Tip

▲ Packets can be assembled and refrigerated several hours before grilling.

Cobb Salad Squares

Prep time: 45 minutes Cook time: 12-15 minutes

All the ingredients of a famous California salad top hot cheesy crusts for these individual "pizzas."

3   cups romaine lettuce, chopped
4   ounces deli turkey breast, cut
      1/2 inch thick
2   plum tomatoes, seeded and
      chopped
1/4   cup (1 ounce) crumbled blue cheese
2   slices crisply-cooked bacon,
      crumbled
1   package (8 ounces) refrigerated
      crescent rolls
2   garlic cloves, pressed
1/2   teaspoon dried basil leaves
4   ounces mozzarella cheese,
      shredded (1 cup)
2   tablespoons Italian salad dressing
2   hard-cooked eggs, sliced

Menu Suggestion

Assemble colorful fresh fruit skewers to accompany these salad squares. Thread fruits such as whole strawberries and grapes, nectarine slices and pineapple chunks on bamboo skewers.

1. Preheat oven to 350°F. Chop lettuce with **Chef's Knife**. Place in **Classic Batter Bowl**. Cut turkey into 1/2-inch cubes. Seed and chop tomatoes. Add turkey, tomatoes, blue cheese and bacon to Batter Bowl; cover and refrigerate.

2. Separate crescent rolls into 4 rectangles on **Rectangle Stone**. Using lightly floured **Dough and Pizza Roller**, press perforations together to seal; roll out dough to make 4 rectangles, 4 x 6 inches. Press garlic over dough using **Garlic Press**; spread evenly with **Skinny Scraper**. Sprinkle with basil. Bake 12-15 minutes or until golden brown. Remove Baking Stone from oven to **Nonstick Cooling Rack**. Immediately top crusts with mozzarella cheese shredded with **Deluxe Cheese Grater**.

3. Toss salad mixture with dressing using **3-Way Tongs**. Place equal amounts of salad mixture over warm crusts. Top with eggs sliced with **Egg Slicer Plus®**. Serve immediately.

Yield: 4 servings

Nutrients per serving: Calories 430, Fat 25 g, Sodium 1310 mg, Dietary Fiber 2 g

Cook's Tips

▲ Hard-cooked eggs can be prepared several days in advance. To hard cook eggs, place eggs in **Petite Saucepan** and fill with enough cold water to cover eggs. Bring water to a boil. Remove saucepan from heat. Cover and let stand 20 minutes. Immediately run cold water into pan to cool eggs. Refrigerate eggs until ready to use.

▲ Add ripe avocado, cut into cubes, to salad mixture, if desired.

Cook's Tip

▲ For added convenience, use a rotisserie-cooked chicken, available at most large supermarkets, for this recipe. One cooked chicken weighs about 2 pounds and will yield approximately 3 cups of diced meat.

Tool Tip

▲ Use the **Crinkle Cutter** to create attractive appetizers. It cuts scalloped edges on vegetables for relish trays and fancy natural cheese slices for cheese and cracker plates.

Make-Ahead Tip

▲ This salad should be made and refrigerated at least 1 hour before serving to allow flavors to blend. Even better, chill it overnight.

Curried Chicken Salad

Prep time: 35 minutes Chill time: 1 hour or overnight

Curry powder, a blend of many spices, is popular in Indian cooking. Just a little gives fruited chicken salad a unique flavor and golden color.

1/2	cup light mayonnaise
1/2	cup low-fat plain yogurt
3/4	teaspoon curry powder
1/4	teaspoon salt
3	cups diced cooked chicken
1 1/2	cups red seedless grapes, cut in half
3/4	cup celery, sliced
1/3	cup green onions with tops, thinly sliced
2	Granny Smith apples
1/3	cup pecans, chopped
1	medium cantaloupe
	Lettuce leaves

Menu Suggestion

Serve salad with crispy *Baked Pita Chips*. Cut pita bread rounds horizontally in half. Cut each half into 8 triangles; place in single layer on flat **Baking Stone**. Bake at 400°F for 8-10 minutes or until lightly browned and crisp.

1. In **Small Batter Bowl**, blend mayonnaise, yogurt, curry powder and salt; set aside.

2. Dice chicken, cut grapes in half and thinly slice celery and green onions using **Chef's Knife**. Core and slice apples using **Apple Peeler/Corer/Slicer**; cut into eighths. Chop pecans with **Food Chopper**. Combine chicken, grapes, celery, green onions, apples and pecans in large **Colander Bowl**. Add mayonnaise mixture; mix lightly with **Mix 'N Scraper®**. Cover with **Colander Bowl Lid**; refrigerate at least 1 hour or overnight.

3. Cut cantaloupe in half lengthwise; remove seeds. Using curved blade of **Grapefruit Knife**, peel rind from melon halves. Place melon halves flat side down on cutting board; cut crosswise into slices using **Crinkle Cutter**. To serve, place cantaloupe slices on lettuce-lined plates; top with chicken mixture.

Yield: 6 servings

Nutrients per serving (about 1 cup salad and 1/6 of melon): Calories 340, Fat 17 g, Sodium 330 mg, Dietary Fiber 3 g

▲ To toast pine nuts, place nuts in **Mini-Baker** and bake at 375°F for 8-10 minutes or until lightly toasted.

▲ Substitute *Vinaigrette Dressing* prepared according to directions on the **Measure, Mix, & Pour™** for bottled red wine vinegar and oil salad dressing, if desired.

Tool Tip

▲ Score cucumber lengthwise with **Lemon Zester/Scorer** and remove seeds with **The Corer™** before slicing, if desired.

Make-Ahead Tip

▲ Several hours before serving, prepare crust and cool completely. Loosely cover crust and let stand at room temperature. Prepare cheese spread and toppers; refrigerate in separate covered containers. Assemble pizza just before serving.

Mediterranean Patio Pizza

Prep time: 45 minutes Cook time: 14-16 minutes

Feta cheese spread and flavorful vegetables top a crust made of bread stick dough. Just one bite transports you to a sunny patio overlooking the sea.

Crust

- 1 package (11 ounces) refrigerated bread sticks
- Olive oil
- 1 garlic clove, pressed

Cheese Spread

- 1 can (14 ounces) artichoke hearts in water, drained, divided
- 4 ounces cream cheese, softened
- 4 ounces feta cheese, crumbled, divided
- 1/2 teaspoon dried oregano leaves

Toppers

- 2 plum tomatoes, seeded and chopped
- 1/3 cup pitted ripe olives, sliced
- 1/3 cup cucumber slices, quartered
- 1/4 small red onion, sliced into thin wedges
- 2 tablespoons pine nuts, toasted (optional)
- 1/4 cup red wine vinegar and oil salad dressing

Menu Suggestion

Plan a casual, pick-up meal with our patio pizza and a cheese and fruit platter. Add a selection of crisp crackers and a sparkling beverage.

1. Preheat oven to 375°F. For crust, unroll bread stick dough; separate into strips. In center of **Classic Round Stone**, coil 1 strip of dough around itself in a spiral pattern. Add second strip to end of first strip and pinch ends; continue coiling dough. Repeat with remaining dough. Using **Dough and Pizza Roller**, roll dough to within 1/2 inch of edge of Baking Stone, pressing seams to seal.

2. Lightly spray dough with olive oil using **Kitchen Spritzer**. Press garlic clove over dough using **Garlic Press**; spread evenly with **Skinny Scraper**. Bake 14-16 minutes or until golden brown; cool completely.

3. For cheese spread, use **Food Chopper** to finely chop enough artichoke hearts to make 1/4 cup. Combine with cream cheese, half of the feta cheese and oregano in **Small Batter Bowl**; mix well. Spread mixture evenly over crust.

4. For toppers, quarter remaining artichoke hearts using **Chef's Knife**. Seed and chop plum tomatoes. Slice olives with **Egg Slicer Plus®**. Using **Ultimate Slice & Grate**, slice cucumber with v-shaped blade; cut slices into quarters. Slice red onion quarter into thin wedges.

5. Arrange vegetables over cream cheese mixture. Sprinkle with remaining feta cheese and pine nuts, if desired. Cut pizza into wedges using **Pizza Cutter**. Drizzle with salad dressing just before serving.

Yield: 6 servings

Nutrients per serving: Calories 350, Fat 19 g, Sodium 930 mg, Dietary Fiber 5 g

Cheesy Chili Casserole

Prep time: 30 minutes Cook time: 30 minutes

When you need to bring a dish to pass, this casual Mexican casserole will satisfy even the heartiest of appetites.

1²/3 cups uncooked elbow macaroni
      (6 ounces)
1   medium green bell pepper,
      chopped
1   medium onion, chopped
1   pound lean (90%) ground beef
1   package (1-1.25 ounces) taco
      seasoning mix
      Water
8   slices (1 ounce each) American
      cheese
1   can (15 ounces) mild chili beans in
      sauce, undrained
1   can (14¹/2 ounces) diced tomatoes,
      undrained
1   cup frozen whole kernel corn
¹/2   teaspoon salt

Menu Suggestion

Bake crusty French bread in our shaped **Bread Tubes** for a special accompaniment. See product leaflet for directions.

1. Preheat oven to 350°F. Cook pasta according to package directions in **4-Qt. Casserole**; drain.

2. Meanwhile, chop bell pepper and onion using **Food Chopper**. Place ground beef, bell pepper and onion in **Family Skillet**. Cook and stir over medium heat 6-7 minutes or until beef is no longer pink; drain. Add taco seasoning mix and amount of water listed on package directions. Continue cooking according to package directions.

3. Cut shapes from cheese slices using any shaped **Bread Tube**; set aside. Chop remaining pieces of cheese using Food Chopper. Combine chopped cheese, macaroni, seasoned meat mixture, chili beans, tomatoes, corn and salt; mix well. Spoon pasta mixture into **Square Baker**.

4. Bake 30 minutes. Top with cheese shapes; continue baking 1-2 minutes or until cheese just begins to melt.

Yield: 8 servings

Nutrients per serving (1¹/4 cups): Calories 440, Fat 20 g, Sodium 1020 mg, Dietary Fiber 6 g

Calico Bean Bake

Prep time: 25 minutes Cook time: 45 minutes

A colorful medley of beans adds interest to a casserole that will feed a crowd but is still easy on the budget.

1/2 pound sliced bacon
1 cup onion, chopped
1 pound lean (90%) ground beef
1 can (28 ounces) cut green beans
1 can (15.5 ounces) red beans
1 can (15.5 ounces) Great Northern beans
1 can (15 ounces) black beans
2 cans (15 ounces each) pork and beans
1 bottle (18 ounces) honey Dijon barbecue sauce

1. Preheat oven to 350°F. Cut bacon into 1-inch pieces using **Chef's Knife**. In **Family Skillet**, cook bacon over medium heat until browned. Remove bacon to paper towels to drain. Discard drippings in pan.

2. Chop onion using **Food Chopper**. Add ground beef and onion to skillet. Cook over medium heat 8-10 minutes or until beef is no longer pink, breaking beef into small crumbles.

3. Meanwhile, drain and rinse all beans except pork and beans in large **Colander**; set aside.

4. Drain beef using small **Colander**; return to skillet. Add reserved beans, undrained pork and beans, barbecue sauce and all except 1/4 cup of the bacon to beef in skillet; mix well.

5. Spoon mixture into **Rectangular Baker**; top with remaining bacon. Bake 45 minutes. Let stand 5 minutes before serving.

Yield: 12 servings

Nutrients per serving (1 cup): Calories 440, Fat 18 g, Sodium 1830 mg, Dietary Fiber 9 g

Mexican Macaroni Medley

Prep time: 20 minutes Cook time: 20 minutes

Making this tasty dish for your next get-together has an added advantage – you can use up those half empty boxes of pasta stored in the pantry.

4 cups (12 ounces) uncooked pasta shapes, such as rotini, elbow, wagon wheel or shell
¼ cup all-purpose flour
1 teaspoon onion powder
2¼ cups milk
1 loaf (8 ounces) prepared cheese product, cubed
1 package (8 ounces) shredded cheddar and Monterey Jack cheese blend, divided
1 can (4 ounces) chopped green chilies, drained
1 medium tomato, seeded and chopped
1 cup chili cheese or barbecue flavor corn chips, coarsely broken

1. Preheat oven to 350°F. Spray **Square Baker** with vegetable oil using **Kitchen Spritzer**. In **Dutch Oven**, bring 4 quarts water to a boil. Add pasta and cook 8-9 minutes or until al denté (tender but firm to the bite). Drain using large **Colander**. Pour into large **Colander Bowl**.

2. Meanwhile, combine flour and onion powder in **Small Saucepan**. Over medium heat, gradually stir in milk using **Nylon Spiral Whisk**. Cook 5-7 minutes or until mixture is as thick as heavy cream, stirring constantly. Remove saucepan from heat. Add cheese product, 1½ cups of the shredded cheese and chilies; stir until cheeses are melted.

3. Mix cheese sauce with pasta using **Classic Scraper**. Spoon into Baker. Top with remaining ½ cup shredded cheese. Bake 20 minutes or until bubbly. Top with tomato and corn chips.

Yield: 7 servings

Nutrients per serving (1 cup): Calories 400, Fat 22 g, Sodium 860 mg, Dietary Fiber 2 g

Kitchen Tips

Cook's Tips

▲ Prepared cheese product is a pasteurized blend of natural cheeses and milk solids. Available in loaves, it is shelf stable (until opening) but usually found near refrigerated cheeses in the supermarket. When melted, it adds a creamy, velvety texture to sauces.

▲ Always add the cheese after you remove the sauce from the heat. This keeps the cheese from getting too hot and curdling.

▲ Measure flour carefully. Too much flour will make this sauce too thick, while too little will make it thin and watery.

Tool Tip

▲ Use the **Stoneware Carrier** to transport this dish to your gathering. Roll up **Oven Pads** or clean kitchen towels and place around **Square Baker** to keep it from shifting in the Carrier.

Cook's Tip

▲ Use leftover ham, deli ham or a ham steak for this casserole. Even turkey ham is a fine choice.

Tool Tips

▲ Use the **Vegetable Peeler** to peel potatoes for this dish, if you prefer.

▲ You'll find a big advantage to using stoneware is that it retains heat after baking. Our attractive **Oval Baker**, made of glazed stoneware, will keep these potatoes warm on the potluck table for a long time.

Double Potato Scallop

Prep time: 20 minutes Cook time: 1 hour, 5 minutes to 1 hour, 10 minutes

Old-fashioned comfort foods never go out of style. Take these saucy potatoes with ham to your next potluck.

1 cup smoked ham, cubed (8 ounces)
1/3 cup green onions with tops, thinly sliced
1 can (10 3/4 ounces) condensed cream of potato soup
1/2 cup whipping cream
1/2 teaspoon salt
1/8 teaspoon ground black pepper
4 large unpeeled potatoes (about 2 pounds)
1/2 cup seasoned croutons

1. Preheat oven to 350°F. Cube ham and thinly slice green onions with **Chef's Knife**. In **Classic Batter Bowl**, combine ham, onions, soup, cream, salt and black pepper using **Mix 'N Scraper®**; set aside.

2. Thinly slice potatoes into Batter Bowl using **Ultimate Slice & Grate**. Fold potatoes into soup mixture. Pour mixture into **Oval Baker**; cover with aluminum foil.

3. Bake 50 minutes. Remove foil. Using **Deluxe Cheese Grater**, grate croutons over potatoes. Return to oven. Continue baking, uncovered, 15-20 minutes or until potatoes are tender.

Yield: 6 servings

Nutrients per serving: Calories 280, Fat 11 g, Sodium 1060 mg, Dietary Fiber 3 g

Gracious Gatherings

Special Fare for Family & Friends

Beef Ragoût with Polenta p. 98

Cook's Tips

▲ Ragoût (ra-GOO) is the French name for a thick, rich stew with meat, poultry or fish that can be made with or without vegetables.

▲ For extra flavor, add 1 teaspoon **Pantry Lemon Pepper Seasoning Mix** to flour mixture, if desired.

▲ It's best to wear plastic gloves when working with fresh jalapeño peppers. Oils from the seeds and membranes of the peppers can irritate your skin and eyes.

Beef Ragoût with Polenta

Prep time: 35 minutes Cook time: 1 hour, 30 minutes
*While this well-seasoned beef stew slowly bakes, you'll have time
to make a salad and set the table.*

1/2 cup all-purpose flour
  2 teaspoons dried oregano leaves
1 1/2 teaspoons chili powder
  1 teaspoon ground cumin
1/2 teaspoon salt
  2 pounds lean beef stew meat,
     cut into 1-inch pieces
  1 tablespoon vegetable oil
  2 garlic cloves, pressed
  4 large carrots
  1 large onion
  1 large green bell pepper
  1 jalapeño pepper
  1 can (6 ounces) tomato paste
  1 can (14 1/2 ounces) seasoned diced
     tomatoes, undrained
  1 can (14 1/2 ounces) beef broth
1/2 cup water
     Polenta (page 99)

1. Preheat oven to 350°F. In **Classic Batter Bowl**, combine flour, oregano, chili powder, cumin and salt. Add beef. Cover bowl with Lid; shake to coat beef.

2. Heat oil in **Family Skillet** over medium-high heat until hot. Press garlic into oil using **Garlic Press**. Add beef to skillet, reserving any remaining flour mixture. Cook beef until evenly browned, stirring occasionally. Remove from heat.

3. Meanwhile, using **Crinkle Cutter**, cut carrots diagonally into 2-inch pieces, then lengthwise in half. Using **Chef's Knife**, cut onion and bell pepper lengthwise into 3/4-inch-thick wedges. Cut jalapeño pepper in half and remove seeds. Chop with **Food Chopper**. Place carrots, onion and peppers in **Stoneware Baking Bowl**. Top with beef; sprinkle with any reserved flour mixture. Spread tomato paste over beef using **Skinny Scraper**. Pour tomatoes, broth and water over beef. Cover with **Deep Dish Baker**.

4. Bake 1 hour and 30 minutes or until beef and vegetables are tender. Meanwhile, prepare *Polenta*. Carefully remove Deep Dish Baker from Baking Bowl, lifting away from you. Spoon ragoût over wedges of polenta.

Yield: 8 servings

LIGHT Nutrients per serving (1 1/4 cups ragoût, 1/8 polenta): Calories 440, Fat 12 g, Sodium 1170 mg, Dietary Fiber 4 g

Polenta

Prep time: 15 minutes Stand time: 30 minutes

Try this traditional Italian side dish in place of potatoes or rice. For creamy polenta, serve immediately or, follow this recipe for a soft but firmer texture that can be sliced.

5   cups water
1½ cups yellow cornmeal
1½ teaspoons salt

Menu Suggestion

Serve with a traditional tossed green salad or, for a flavorful twist, serve mixed greens with fresh pear slices, crumbled blue cheese, toasted chopped walnuts and balsamic vinaigrette dressing.

1. In **Medium Saucepan**, bring water to a boil over high heat. Slowly whisk in cornmeal and salt using **Nylon Spiral Whisk**. Return mixture to a boil. Reduce heat to low; partially cover with saucepan lid to reduce spattering. Simmer 8-10 minutes or until mixture is very thick, stirring occasionally. Remove Saucepan from heat.

2. Spray **Springform Pan** with vegetable oil using **Kitchen Spritzer**. Pour cornmeal mixture into pan, spreading evenly. Let cool at room temperature until firm (about 30 minutes). Let stand at room temperature until ready to serve. Cut into 8 wedges using **Slice 'N Serve®**.

Yield: 8 servings

Cook's Tips
▲ Save 120 calories
and 17 grams of fat
per serving by
substituting fat-free
evaporated milk for
whipping cream.

▲ The thinner the
asparagus spear, the
more tender it will be.
If spears are thick, cut
in half lengthwise.

▲ Substitute 1
teaspoon dried basil
leaves for fresh, if
desired. Add dried basil
to whipping cream
during heating.

Creamy Pasta with Spring Vegetables

Prep time: 35 minutes Cook time: 20-25 minutes

*A medley of roasted vegetables is tossed with pasta, heavy cream and fresh basil.
Finish with a sprinkling of fresh Parmesan cheese.*

8 ounces thin fresh asparagus spears

8 ounces baby portobello or medium white button mushrooms

1 large red bell pepper

2 tablespoons olive oil

3 garlic cloves, pressed

1/4 teaspoon salt

1/4 teaspoon coarsely ground black pepper

2 tablespoons fresh basil leaves, snipped

8 ounces (about 3 cups) uncooked rigatoni (pasta tubes with ridges)

3/4 cup whipping cream

2 ounces fresh Parmesan cheese, grated (about 1/2 cup)

Menu Suggestion

Complete your menu with a crisp green salad and crusty French bread.

1. Preheat oven to 425°F. Snap off and discard tough ends of asparagus. Cut into 1½-inch pieces. Cut mushrooms in half (or quarters if large). Cut bell pepper into 1-inch squares. Combine vegetables in large **Colander Bowl**. Add olive oil and mix lightly. Press garlic over vegetables using **Garlic Press**. Add salt and black pepper; mix well. Pour into **Stoneware Bar Pan**. Bake 10-12 minutes or until vegetables are crisp-tender.

2. Meanwhile, snip basil with **Kitchen Shears**; set aside. Prepare pasta according to package directions in **4-Qt. Casserole**. In **Petite Saucepan**, simmer whipping cream 6-8 minutes over medium-low heat to thicken slightly, stirring constantly with **Nylon Spiral Whisk**.

3. Drain pasta in large **Colander**. Transfer to large **Colander Bowl**. Add vegetables, heated cream and basil. Mix lightly using **Nylon Slotted Server**.

4. Using **Deluxe Cheese Grater**, grate half of the Parmesan cheese into pasta mixture; mix lightly. Spoon onto serving plates. Sprinkle with additional black pepper and remaining grated cheese.

Yield: 4 servings

Nutrients per serving: Calories 390, Fat 28 g, Sodium 380 mg, Dietary Fiber 3 g

Elegant Chicken Rolls

Prep time: 45 minutes   Cook time: 35 minutes

*Feta cheese spread, roasted red peppers, fresh spinach leaves and smoked ham
are baked inside crumb-coated chicken breasts.*

6	boneless, skinless chicken breast halves (4-6 ounces each)
4	ounces cream cheese, softened
4	ounces crumbled feta cheese
2	tablespoons fresh basil leaves, snipped
1/2	teaspoon coarsely ground black pepper
6	tablespoons sweet roasted red peppers, drained and chopped
1¼	cups seasoned croutons, grated (1 cup crumbs)
1	egg
1	tablespoon milk
12-18	large spinach leaves
6	ounces thinly sliced deli smoked ham

Menu Suggestion

Impress your dinner guests with these fancy chicken rolls, rice pilaf, sugar snap peas and miniature croissants or crusty French bread slices.

1. Preheat oven to 375°F. Butterfly cut each chicken breast half with **Quikut Paring Knife** by inserting tip of knife into thickest side of chicken then cutting lengthwise through middle of breast, almost through to the other side. Spread chicken breast open flat. Place each chicken breast between 2 pieces of **Parchment Paper**. Flatten chicken to at least ¼ inch thickness by alternately pounding and rolling with **Dough and Pizza Roller**; set aside.

2. In **Small Batter Bowl**, combine cream cheese, feta cheese, basil snipped with the **Kitchen Shears** and black pepper; blend well and set aside. Chop red peppers with **Food Chopper**; drain on paper towels.

3. Grate croutons using coarse grating drum of **Deluxe Cheese Grater** into shallow bowl. Combine egg and milk in **Classic Batter Bowl** using **Stainless Steel Whisk**.

4. For each chicken roll, cover chicken breast with single layer of spinach leaves. Using **Medium Scoop**, top with scoop of cheese mixture; spread to within ¼ inch of edge using **All-Purpose Spreader**. Sprinkle evenly with 1 tablespoon of the red peppers and cover with 2 slices of the ham. Roll up, jelly-roll fashion, tucking in ends when possible.

5. Dip rolls in egg mixture; coat with crumbs. Place seam side down in **Square Baker**. Bake 35 minutes or until chicken is no longer pink and juices run clear.

Yield: 6 servings

Nutrients per serving: Calories 490, Fat 20 g, Sodium 890 mg, Dietary Fiber less than 1 g

Kitchen Tips

Cook's Tip

▲ For ease in cutting chicken, place in freezer about 30 minutes or until slightly firm.

Make-Ahead Tip

▲ Chicken rolls can be prepared, except for coating with crumbs, up to 2 hours before baking. Cover and refrigerate. When ready to serve, dip rolls in egg mixture and coat with crumbs as recipe directs. Bake at 375°F for 35-45 minutes or until chicken is no longer pink and juices run clear.

Cook's Tips

▲ Substitute condensed cream of celery soup for shrimp soup, if desired.

▲ Using whole milk ricotta cheese will add extra richness and creaminess to this lasagna but part-skim ricotta works fine too.

Make-Ahead Tip

▲ Assemble lasagna, cover and refrigerate. When ready to bake, remove from refrigerator while preheating oven. Increase covered baking time 10 minutes.

Seafood Lasagna

Prep time: 55 minutes   Cook time: 45-50 minutes

This colorful, seafood and vegetable lasagna takes time to assemble, but once it's in the oven a hostess can mingle with guests.

9   uncooked lasagna noodles
1   can (10¾ ounces) condensed cream of shrimp soup
¼   cup milk
1   container (15 ounces) ricotta cheese
1   egg
1   ounce fresh Parmesan cheese, grated (about ¼ cup)
5   tablespoons fresh parsley, snipped, divided
¼   teaspoon ground black pepper
1½ cups green onions with tops, sliced
1   cup red bell pepper, chopped
1   teaspoon olive oil
4   garlic cloves, pressed
12 ounces frozen, cooked medium shrimp, thawed
1   package (8 ounces) flake- or chunk-style imitation crabmeat
3   cups (12 ounces) shredded mozzarella cheese

1. Preheat oven to 350°F. Cook noodles according to package directions in **Dutch Oven**; drain. Mix soup and milk in **Small Batter Bowl**; set aside.

2. In **Classic Batter Bowl**, mix ricotta cheese and egg. Using **Deluxe Cheese Grater**, grate Parmesan cheese into Batter Bowl. Snip parsley using **Kitchen Shears**. Reserve 1 tablespoon. Add remaining

4 tablespoons parsley and black pepper to Batter Bowl; mix well and set aside.

3. Slice green onions with **Chef's Knife**. Chop bell pepper using **Food Chopper**. Heat oil in **Large Skillet** over medium heat. Add green onions, bell pepper and garlic pressed with **Garlic Press**; cook and stir 2-3 minutes or until tender. Remove pan from heat. Cut each shrimp crosswise in half. Coarsely flake crabmeat. Add seafood to vegetables.

4. To assemble lasagna, spread ¼ cup of the soup mixture over bottom of **Rectangular Baker**. Top with 3 noodles. Spread half of the ricotta mixture over noodles. Sprinkle with half of the vegetable-seafood mixture and 1 cup of the mozzarella cheese. Repeat layers of noodles, ricotta mixture, vegetable-seafood mixture and mozzarella cheese. Top with remaining 3 noodles. Spread with remaining soup mixture; sprinkle with remaining cheese.

5. Cover Baker with **Rectangular Lid/Bowl**. Bake 35 minutes. Carefully remove Lid/Bowl, lifting away from you. Continue baking 10-15 minutes or until hot and bubbly. Remove from oven; sprinkle with reserved parsley. Let stand 15 minutes. Cut into squares; serve using **Large Serving Spatula**.

Yield: 12 servings

Nutrients per serving: Calories 270, Fat 11 g, Sodium 550 mg, Dietary Fiber 1 g

Pork Chops with Harvest Stuffing

Prep time: 50 minutes   Cook time: 50-55 minutes

Our Rectangular Baker and Lid/Bowl team up to make these pork chops tender and juicy.

8 boneless pork loin chops, 3/4 inch thick (about 6 ounces each)
1 cup celery, chopped
3/4 cup onion, chopped
1/4 cup fresh parsley, snipped
1 package (16 ounces) corn bread stuffing mix
2-21/4 cups water
1 cup dried cranberries
1/4 cup butter or margarine, melted
1 teaspoon dried thyme leaves
1 teaspoon salt
1/4 teaspoon ground black pepper
1 tablespoon vegetable oil, divided
1/2 cup orange marmalade

Menu Suggestion

Serve with cooked broccoli spears and a fresh apple salad or chunky applesauce.

1. Preheat oven to 350°F. Trim excess fat from chops using **Utility Knife**. For each chop, insert tip of knife in center of one long side and cut a small pocket.

2. Chop celery and onion using **Food Chopper**; place in large **Colander Bowl**. Snip parsley with **Kitchen Shears**. Add to bowl along with stuffing mix, water, cranberries and butter; mix lightly using **Mix 'N Scraper®**.

3. Using **Medium Scoop**, place one rounded scoop stuffing in pocket of each chop. Close pockets with wooden picks placed crisscross over openings. Spoon remaining stuffing into **Rectangular Baker**. Rub both sides of chops with combined seasonings.

4. Heat **Family Skillet** over medium-high heat. Add half of oil and 4 chops. Brown chops 1-2 minutes on each side. Remove to Baker. Repeat with remaining oil and chops. Arrange chops over stuffing. Cover with **Rectangular Lid/Bowl**. Bake 40 minutes. Carefully remove Lid/Bowl from Baker.

5. Microwave marmalade in **Small Micro-Cooker®** on HIGH 30 seconds. Spoon marmalade over chops. Continue baking, uncovered, 10-15 minutes or until **Pocket Thermometer** inserted into thickest part of chops registers 160°F. Remove picks.

Yield: 8 servings

Nutrients per serving: Calories 760, Fat 27 g, Sodium 1090 mg, Dietary Fiber 4 g

Cook's Tips

▲ Place chops in freezer about 10 minutes for meat to firm. This will make it easier to cut pockets.

▲ Substitute raisins or dried cherries for cranberries, if desired.

Make-Ahead Tip

▲ Stuffing mixture can be prepared in advance and refrigerated, but stuff chops, brown and bake just before serving.

Cook's Tips

▲ Substitute 1 teaspoon dried dill weed for All-Purpose Dill Mix, if desired.

▲ Cook and chop 3 boneless, skinless chicken breast halves to get 2 cups of chopped cooked chicken.

▲ It's best to keep crescent roll dough refrigerated until ready to use. Once the dough is warm, it becomes soft and sometimes sticky, making it difficult to work with.

Tool Tip

▲ When you're making pies and pizzas, you'll find our **Dough and Pizza Roller** is easier to use than a traditional rolling pin. It's designed for one-handed use, and the compact rollers allow you to spread dough right on flat Baking Stones and in Bakers.

Chicken & Broccoli Braid

Prep time: 25 minutes Cook time: 25-28 minutes

This impressive braid is filled with a cheesy combination of chicken and crisp vegetables.

2 cups cooked chicken, chopped
1 cup broccoli, chopped
1/2 cup red bell pepper, chopped
1 garlic clove, pressed
4 ounces sharp cheddar cheese, shredded (1 cup)
1/2 cup mayonnaise
2 teaspoons Pantry All-Purpose Dill Mix
1/4 teaspoon salt
2 packages (8 ounces each) refrigerated crescent rolls
1 egg white, lightly beaten
2 tablespoons slivered almonds

Menu Suggestion

For the perfect brunch, serve this braid with a Bibb lettuce and fresh fruit salad drizzled with poppy seed dressing and miniature caramel pecan rolls.

1. Preheat oven to 375°F. Chop chicken and broccoli using **Food Chopper**; place in **Classic Batter Bowl**. Chop bell pepper using **Utility Knife**; add to Batter Bowl. Press garlic over vegetable mixture using **Garlic Press**.

2. Shred cheese using **Deluxe Cheese Grater** and add to vegetable mixture; mix gently. Add mayonnaise, Dill Mix and salt; mix well using **Mix 'N Scraper®**.

3. Unroll 1 package of crescent dough; do not separate. Arrange longest sides of dough across width of **Rectangle Stone**. Repeat with remaining package of dough. Using **Dough and Pizza Roller**, roll dough to seal perforations. On longest sides of Baking Stone, cut dough into strips 1 1/2 inches apart, 3 inches deep using **Paring Knife**. (There will be 6 inches in the center for the filling.)

4. Spread filling evenly over middle of dough. To braid, lift strips of dough across mixture to meet in center, twisting each strip one turn. Continue alternating strips to form a braid. Tuck ends up to seal at end of braid.

5. Brush egg white over dough using **Pastry Brush**. Sprinkle with almonds. Bake 25-28 minutes or until deep golden brown. Cut and serve using **Slice 'N Serve®**.

Yield: 10 servings

Nutrients per serving: Calories 410, Fat 27 g, Sodium 660 mg, Dietary Fiber less than 1 g

Hunter's Beef Pot Pie

Prep time: 45 minutes   Cook time: 13-15 minutes

*Tender beef, mushrooms, potatoes and carrots bake in a seasoned sauce
under a golden brown bread lattice.*

Beef Mixture

- 1 fully cooked, ready-to-eat boneless beef pot roast with gravy (about 2 pounds)
- 4 slices bacon
- 1 cup baby carrots
- 2 cups refrigerated diced potatoes with onion
- 1 pound mushrooms
- 2 garlic cloves, pressed

Sauce

- 2 tablespoons cornstarch
- 1 can (14 1/2 ounces) beef broth, divided
- 2 teaspoons fresh snipped rosemary or 1 teaspoon dried rosemary
- 2 teaspoons balsamic vinegar
  Salt and ground black pepper to taste (optional)

Topping

- 2 tablespoons butter, melted
- 1 tablespoon fresh parsley, snipped
- 1 garlic clove, pressed
- 1 package (11 ounces) refrigerated bread sticks

1. Preheat oven to 400°F. For beef mixture, remove pot roast from gravy, reserving gravy (about 1 cup). Cut beef into 1/2-inch cubes with **Chef's Knife**; set aside.

2. Finely chop bacon; cook in **Family Skillet** over medium heat until crisp; remove bacon to paper towels. Reserve 2 tablespoons drippings in skillet.

3. Cut carrots lengthwise in half with **Paring Knife**. Cook carrots and potatoes in reserved bacon drippings over medium heat 8 minutes, stirring occasionally. Slice mushrooms with **Egg Slicer Plus®** and press garlic with **Garlic Press**. Add to skillet and continue cooking 8-10 minutes or until vegetables are crisp-tender, stirring occasionally. Stir in reserved beef cubes and bacon.

4. Meanwhile, for sauce, whisk cornstarch into 1/4 cup broth in **Petite Saucepan** using **Nylon Spiral Whisk**. Gradually whisk in remaining broth, reserved gravy, rosemary and balsamic vinegar. Bring to a boil over medium heat. Boil 1 minute, stirring constantly, until thickened. Season to taste with salt and black pepper. Add sauce to meat mixture. Heat thoroughly, stirring frequently. Pour into **Oval Baker**.

5. For topping, melt butter in **Small Micro-Cooker®**. Add parsley snipped with **Kitchen Shears** and garlic. Unroll bread sticks; do not separate. Press middle perforation together. Separate into 6 long strips. Twist strips and place diagonally over top of Baker in a lattice fashion. Brush with butter mixture using **Pastry Brush**.

6. Bake 13-15 minutes until beef mixture is bubbly and topping is golden brown.

Yield: 8 servings

Nutrients per serving: Calories 380, Fat 12 g, Sodium 1030 mg, Dietary Fiber 3 g

Cook's Tips

▲ Salmon is often sold in large fillets (1-2 pounds) with the skin intact. At the fish counter, you can ask to have the skin removed and the fillet cut into individual portions. To remove the skin yourself, place fillet, skin side down, on cutting board. At one end, cut through to the skin using **Chef's Knife**. While firmly holding onto the skin, angle the knife and cut the flesh from the skin using a sawing motion.

▲ You'll find prepared basil pesto in the refrigerated fresh pasta or Italian foods section of the supermarket. It is a flavorful sauce made with basil, garlic, pine nuts, Parmesan cheese and olive oil.

Make-Ahead Tip

▲ Salmon packets can be made 1-2 hours in advance and refrigerated. Remove packets from refrigerator while preheating your oven. Increase baking time 2-3 minutes.

Salmon en Papillote

Prep time: 30 minutes Cook time: 13-15 minutes

Cooking fish en papillote [pah-pee-YOHT] refers to the French method of baking fish in a wrapping of parchment paper.

- 2/3 **cup uncooked orzo pasta**
- 2 **plum tomatoes**
- 1/4 **cup green onions with tops, sliced**
- 1/3 **cup pitted ripe olives, sliced**
- 3 **tablespoons prepared basil pesto, divided**
- 1/2 **teaspoon lemon zest**
- 1/4 **teaspoon salt**
- 4 **skinless salmon fillets (4-6 ounces each)**

Menu Suggestion

Serve with fresh whole green beans, steamed and tossed with pressed garlic sautéed in olive oil, and fresh fruit cups.

1. Preheat oven to 425°F. Cut four 15-inch squares of **Parchment Paper** using **Kitchen Shears**. Fold in half and cut to make large heart shapes when unfolded.

2. Cook pasta according to package directions; drain in small **Colander**. Place pasta in small **Colander Bowl**. Cut tomatoes lengthwise in half using **Chef's Knife**; remove seeds. Chop tomatoes. Slice green onions. Slice olives using **Egg Slicer Plus®**. Add tomatoes, green onions, olives and 1 tablespoon of the pesto to pasta. Prepare lemon zest using **Lemon Zester/Scorer**. Stir lemon zest and salt into pasta mixture. Rinse salmon with cold running water; pat dry.

3. For each serving, open paper heart and spoon about 3/4 cup pasta mixture on right side; top with salmon fillet. Spread salmon with 1 1/2 teaspoons of the remaining pesto using **All-Purpose Spreader**. Fold left side of heart over salmon. Starting at top, tightly seal packet by making a series of short, narrow, overlapping folds along the open edge. At bottom of heart twist tip and turn up.

4. Arrange packets on **Stoneware Bar Pan**. Bake 13-15 minutes. (Carefully open one packet to test that salmon flakes easily with fork.) Immediately remove packets from Bar Pan using **Large Serving Spatula**. To serve, cut an "X" through top layer of paper and fold back points.

Yield: 4 servings

Nutrients per serving: Calories 570, Fat 26 g, Sodium 430 mg, Dietary Fiber 2 g

Florentine Shells

Prep time: 40 minutes Cook time: 45 minutes

*Many guests enjoy meatless entrées. These savory, spinach-stuffed shells
are baked in a rich, creamy tomato sauce.*

18 uncooked jumbo pasta shells
 1 container (15 ounces) part-skim
    ricotta cheese
 1 package (10 ounces) frozen chopped
    spinach, thawed, drained and
    squeezed dry
 2 cups (8 ounces) shredded Italian
    cheese blend, divided
3/4 cup half-and-half, divided
 1 ounce fresh Parmesan cheese, grated
    (about 1/4 cup)
 1 garlic clove, pressed
1/2 teaspoon dried basil leaves
1/2 teaspoon dried oregano leaves
1/8 teaspoon salt
 1 jar (26-28 ounces) spaghetti sauce

Menu Suggestion

Serve with cooked asparagus
spears, a crisp green salad and
warm garlic bread. Enjoy Italian
ice or biscotti cookies with coffee
for dessert.

1. Preheat oven to 350°F. Cook pasta shells
   according to package directions; drain.

2. Meanwhile, in **Classic Batter Bowl**,
   combine ricotta cheese, spinach, 1 1/2 cups
   of the Italian cheese blend and 1/4 cup of
   the half-and-half. Grate Parmesan cheese
   into Batter Bowl using **Deluxe Cheese
   Grater**. Press garlic into Bowl using **Garlic
   Press**. Add seasonings; mix well and set
   aside.

3. In **Small Batter Bowl**, whisk spaghetti
   sauce and remaining 1/2 cup half-and-half
   with **Stainless Steel Whisk** until blended.
   Reserve 1 cup of the sauce mixture; spread
   remaining sauce mixture over bottom
   of **Rectangular Baker**. Using **Medium
   Scoop**, fill each shell with rounded scoop
   of spinach mixture. Arrange filled shells in
   Baker. Top evenly with reserved sauce
   mixture. Cover Baker with **Rectangular
   Lid/Bowl**.

4. Bake, covered, 40 minutes. Remove
   Lid/Bowl. Sprinkle shells with remaining
   1/2 cup Italian cheese blend. Continue
   baking, uncovered, 5 minutes or until
   cheese is melted. Remove from oven; let
   stand 10 minutes.

Yield: 6 servings

Nutrients per serving (3 shells): Calories 600, Fat 29 g,
Sodium 1720 mg, Dietary Fiber 5 g

Cook's Tips

▲ If using a charcoal grill, light charcoal briquettes and allow about 30 minutes for coals to reach a medium cooking temperature. The surface of the coals will be ash-covered. Coals should be spread in a single layer. If using a gas grill, consult the owner's manual for heating directions.

▲ It's easy to see long fibers that run the length of the flank steak. When carving, you'll want to cut the meat into thin strips diagonally across these fibers (the grain) in order to get tender pieces of meat.

▲ For **Chicken Fajitas**, substitute 6 boneless, skinless chicken breast halves (4-6 ounces each) for steak. Marinate 1 hour. Grill chicken and vegetables at medium temperature 12-15 minutes or until chicken is no longer pink and vegetables are tender, turning occasionally. (Note: Vegetables may take longer to cook than chicken.)

Patio Party Fajitas

Prep time: 15 minutes Marinating time: 6-8 hours or overnight
Grill time: 17-21 minutes

A spicy citrus marinade not only tenderizes beef flank steak but gives it lots of zip.

Marinade

- 1/2 **cup lime juice**
- 1/4 **cup vegetable oil**
- 3-4 **medium jalapeño peppers**
- 3 **garlic cloves, pressed**
- 3 **tablespoons fresh cilantro, snipped**
- 2 **teaspoons chili powder**
- 1/2 **teaspoon ground cumin**
- 1/4 **teaspoon salt**

Fajitas

- 1 **beef flank steak (1 1/2-2 pounds)**
- 2 **medium green bell peppers**
- 6 **sweet onion slices, cut 1/2 inch thick**
- 12 **(6-7 inch) flour tortillas**
  Optional Toppings: salsa, shredded Mexican cheese blend, sliced pitted ripe olives and sour cream

Menu Suggestion

Treat your guests to Tex-Mex trimmings. Add refried beans or Mexican rice. Or, mix up a black bean-corn relish seasoned with green onions, cilantro and Italian salad dressing. Add a fresh fruit platter and citrus punch.

1. For marinade, combine lime juice and oil in **Small Batter Bowl**. Cut jalapeño peppers in half lengthwise; carefully remove seeds and membranes. (See Cook's Tip, page 98). Chop finely with **Food Chopper**. Add to Batter Bowl along with garlic pressed with **Garlic Press**, cilantro snipped with **Kitchen Shears** and remaining marinade ingredients; mix well.

2. Place steak and marinade in resealable plastic food storage bag; turn to coat. Marinate in refrigerator 6-8 hours or overnight, turning occasionally.

3. For fajitas, prepare grill for cooking at medium temperature. Cut bell peppers into quarters; remove membranes and seeds. Remove steak from marinade; discard marinade. Place steak, bell peppers and onions on grid of grill. Grill, uncovered, 17-21 minutes or until steak is medium rare (145°F) to medium (160°F) doneness and vegetables are tender, turning occasionally using **Bar-B-Tongs** and **Bar-B-Boss**. Remove steak and vegetables from grill.

4. Wrap tortillas in heavy-duty aluminum foil; grill 5-7 minutes to warm. Cut bell peppers into strips and onion slices in half. Carve steak diagonally across the grain into thin slices. To serve, place steak and vegetable slices in center of each tortilla. Top with salsa, cheese, ripe olives and sour cream, if desired.

Yield: 6 servings

Nutrients per serving (2 fajitas): Calories 550, Fat 25 g, Sodium 710 mg, Dietary Fiber 3 g

Italian Sausage Charlotte

Prep time: 30 minutes Cook time: 25-30 minutes

This contemporary casserole, featured on our cover, is a savory twist on a French classic.
It pairs custard-dipped bread slices that bake up crispy over a zesty filling.

Meat Mixture
- 1½ pounds mild Italian sausage links
- 1 medium zucchini, sliced
- 8 ounces mushrooms, sliced
- 1 medium red or green bell pepper
- 1 jar (16 ounces) white Alfredo pasta sauce, divided

Topping
- ½ cup milk
- 2 eggs
- 1 garlic clove, pressed
- 2 teaspoons Pantry Italian Seasoning Mix, divided
- ⅛ teaspoon salt
- 16 slices firm white bread
- 1 can (14½ ounces) diced tomatoes, drained
- 2 tablespoons fresh Parmesan cheese, grated

Menu Suggestion

Accompany this savory Italian dish with a romaine lettuce salad topped with tomato wedges, quartered marinated artichoke hearts, pitted ripe olives and *Caesar Dressing* made in our **Measure, Mix, & Pour™**. Grate fresh Parmesan cheese over top.

1. Preheat oven to 400°F. For meat mixture, remove casings from sausage links; discard casings. Cut sausages crosswise into ½-inch pieces. Cook sausage in **Stir-Fry Skillet** over medium heat until well browned and no longer pink, turning with **Nylon Turner** as meat browns.

2. Meanwhile, using **Ultimate Slice & Grate**, slice zucchini using v-shaped blade. Slice mushrooms with **Egg Slicer Plus®**. Cut red bell pepper into ¼-inch strips. Remove sausage from skillet; drain well on paper towels. Wipe out skillet with paper towels and add 1 cup of the Alfredo sauce; bring to a boil. Stir in sausage and vegetables. Pour mixture into **Oval Baker**, mounding slightly in the center.

3. For topping, in **Small Batter Bowl**, whisk together remaining Alfredo sauce, milk and eggs using **Stainless Steel Whisk**. Add garlic pressed with **Garlic Press**, 1 teaspoon of the Seasoning Mix and salt. Cut crusts off bread using **Serrated Bread Knife**. Dip bread into egg mixture, coating lightly; overlap bread in a circular pattern over sausage mixture, leaving center open.

4. Drain tomatoes in small **Colander**; transfer to small **Colander Bowl**. Add remaining 1 teaspoon Seasoning Mix; mix with **Mix 'N Scraper®**. Spoon tomato mixture into opening. Using **Deluxe Cheese Grater**, grate cheese over top. Bake 25-30 minutes or until edges of bread are deep golden brown.

Yield: 8 servings

Nutrients per serving: Calories 640, Fat 42 g, Sodium 1460 mg, Dietary Fiber 3 g

Kitchen Tips

Cook's Tips

▲ When adding milk to softened cream cheese, add it very gradually while whisking with the **Stainless Steel Whisk** to keep the mixture smooth and free of lumps.

▲ Lifting up on **Parchment Paper** will help make the baked omelet roll up. Be sure to remove the paper as you are rolling.

Ham & Cheese Omelet Roll

Prep time: 15 minutes Cook time: 30-33 minutes

This brunch specialty combines ham, cheese and green onions rolled into a soufflé-like omelet.

- 4 ounces cream cheese, softened
- 3/4 cup milk
- 2 tablespoons all-purpose flour
- 1/4 teaspoon salt
- 12 eggs
- 8 ounces ham, finely chopped (1 1/2 cups)
- 6 ounces cheddar or Swiss cheese, shredded (1 1/2 cups)
- 1/4 cup green onions with tops, thinly sliced
- 2 tablespoons Dijon mustard

Menu Suggestion

Complete your brunch with spicy tomato juice, fruit salad, warm muffins or bagels and fresh brewed coffee.

1. Preheat oven to 375°F. In **Small Batter Bowl**, combine cream cheese and milk; whisk until smooth using **Stainless Steel Whisk**. Add flour and salt; whisk to combine.

2. In **Classic Batter Bowl**, gently whisk eggs until blended. Add cream cheese mixture; mix well.

3. Cut an 18-inch long piece of **Parchment Paper**. Press into bottom and up sides of **Stoneware Bar Pan** to prevent egg mixture from running under parchment paper; pinch corners. Pour egg mixture into bottom of Bar Pan. Bake 30-33 minutes or until omelet is puffy and golden.

4. Meanwhile, finely chop ham using **Food Chopper**. Shred cheese using **Deluxe Cheese Grater**. Thinly slice green onions with **Chef's Knife**.

5. Remove omelet from oven; immediately spread with Dijon mustard using **Skinny Scraper**. Sprinkle with half of the cheese; top with ham and green onions. Sprinkle with remaining cheese. Starting at one short side, roll up jelly-roll fashion, removing parchment paper as you roll. Garnish top with additional cheese and green onions, if desired. Let stand 5 minutes to allow cheese to melt. Slice roll diagonally into wedges using **Serrated Bread Knife**.

Yield: 8 servings

Nutrients per serving: Calories 300, Fat 20 g, Sodium 760 mg, Dietary Fiber 0 g

Grilled Steaks with Savory Butters

Prep time: 20 minutes   Grill time: 6-8 minutes

Add sizzle to your summer with these juicy ribeye steaks, served hot off the grill with herb butter toppers.

Blue Cheese and Herb Butter

- 1/4 cup butter, softened
- 2 tablespoons crumbled blue cheese
- 2 teaspoons chopped green onion with top
- 1/2 teaspoon fresh lemon juice
- 1/4 teaspoon coarsely ground black pepper

Steaks

- 4 garlic cloves, pressed
- 4 beef ribeye steaks, cut 3/4 inch thick (about 8 ounces each)
- 1/2 teaspoon salt
- 1/2 teaspoon coarsely ground black pepper

Menu Suggestion

Grilled vegetables are a wonderful accompaniment to these steaks. Traditionalists may prefer baked potatoes and tossed salads.

1. For Blue Cheese and Herb Butter, place butter and blue cheese in **Small Batter Bowl**. Add green onion, lemon juice and coarsely ground black pepper ground with **Salt and Pepper Mill**; mix until well blended.

2. Prepare grill for cooking at medium temperature. For steaks, press garlic cloves using **Garlic Press**. Spread garlic evenly over both sides of steaks using **All-Purpose Spreader**. Sprinkle both sides with salt and black pepper.

3. Place steaks on grid of grill. Grill, uncovered, 6-8 minutes for medium rare (145°F) to medium (160°F) doneness, turning occasionally using **Bar-B-Tongs**. Top steaks with Blue Cheese and Herb Butter.

Yield: 4 servings

Nutrients per serving: Calories 480, Fat 31 g, Sodium 540 mg, Dietary Fiber 0 g

Variations: **Chipotle Herb Butter:** Combine 1/4 cup softened butter, 1 teaspoon pressed chipotle chile peppers, 1 teaspoon snipped fresh cilantro and 1/4 teaspoon salt; mix until well blended.

Peppered Herb Butter: Combine 1/4 cup softened butter, 2 teaspoons snipped fresh chives, 1/2 teaspoon snipped fresh rosemary, 1/2 teaspoon fresh lemon juice and 1/4 teaspoon coarsely ground black pepper; mix until well blended.

Kitchen Tips

Cook's Tips

▲ Herb butters are also delicious when served on baked potatoes, grilled corn on the cob or hot vegetables.

▲ For tips on preparing your grill for cooking, see page 116.

▲ Look for canned chipotles in adobo sauce in the Mexican foods section of your supermarket. The small chile pepper is actually a dried, smoked jalapeño pepper. Use the **Garlic Press** to press the peppers; discard skin and seeds.

Tool Tips

▲ Use the **Kitchen Shears** to snip fresh herbs for herb butters.

▲ When serving steaks, bring out your **Pampered Chef Steak Knife Set**. These quality knives come in a special case featuring a sharpening and honing system enabling you to always keep them sharp.

Cook's Tips

▲ The buttered **Parchment Paper** "cover" bastes the fish and keeps it moist while baking.

▲ Most trout available at fish counters is farm-raised. Trout has a mild, nutty flavor and tender flesh. When buying whole trout, look for bright, clear eyes and skin that is shiny and moist. Store trout by wrapping tightly and placing in the coldest part of your refrigerator. Use it within two days.

Make-Ahead Tip

▲ Rice mixture can be made up to a day in advance, but stuff trout shortly before guests arrive. Be sure to refrigerate stuffed trout until baking. Remove Bar Pan from refrigerator while oven is preheating.

Backwoods Stuffed Trout

Prep time: 1 hour, 20 minutes Cook time: 25 minutes

This fish has a certain rustic appeal with its nutty wild rice stuffing.

1 package (4 ounces) uncooked wild rice (²/₃ cup)

¼ cup slivered almonds

½ cup onion, chopped

½ cup celery, chopped

1 tablespoon butter or margarine

1 orange

2 tablespoons fresh parsley, snipped

Salt

Ground black pepper

4 whole trout, cleaned (8-10 ounces each)

Butter, softened

Menu Suggestion

Serve with a quick sauté of mixed vegetables such as zucchini, summer squash and red onion.

1. In **Medium Saucepan**, prepare rice according to package directions except omit salt.

2. Meanwhile, toast almonds in **Large Skillet** over medium-high heat 3-5 minutes, stirring frequently. Remove from pan; cool. Chop with **Food Chopper**. Mix rice and almonds in **Small Batter Bowl**.

3. Chop onion and celery with Food Chopper. Cook in 1 tablespoon butter in frying pan over medium heat 2-3 minutes or until crisp-tender. Add to rice.

4. Zest orange with short strokes of **Lemon Zester/Scorer** to measure 2 teaspoons zest. Squeeze orange to measure ¼ cup juice; reserve 1 tablespoon. Add remaining 3 tablespoons of the juice, zest, parsley snipped with **Kitchen Shears**, ½ teaspoon salt and ⅛ teaspoon black pepper to rice; mix well.

5. Preheat oven to 350°F. Using **Kitchen Spritzer**, lightly spray **Stoneware Bar Pan** with vegetable oil. Rinse trout; pat inside and outside dry. Lightly sprinkle salt and pepper over inside cavities; drizzle with reserved 1 tablespoon juice. Stuff each trout with rice mixture (about ²/₃ cup). Arrange trout in Bar Pan; surround trout with any remaining rice.

6. From roll of **Parchment Paper**, tear off sheet 11 inches long and lightly butter one side. Place buttered side of paper loosely over fish. Bake 25 minutes or until fish flakes easily with a fork.

Yield: 4 servings

Nutrients per serving: Calories 400, Fat 18 g, Sodium 690 mg, Dietary Fiber 2 g

Index

About Our Recipes

All recipes were developed and tested in The Pampered Chef Test Kitchens by professional home economists. Each recipe includes guidelines for preparation and cooking times. As an important first step, we suggest you read through the recipe and assemble the necessary ingredients and equipment. "Prep time" is the approximate amount of time needed to prepare recipe ingredients before a final "Cook time". Prep time includes active steps such as chopping and mixing. It can also include cooking ingredients for a dish that is assembled and then baked or grilled. Some preparation steps can be done simultaneously or during cooking and are usually indicated by the term "meanwhile." Some recipes that can be ready to eat in 30 minutes or less and that have steps not easily separated have a combined "Prep and cook time".

A Note on Nutrition

At the end of each recipe, we list calories, total fat, sodium and dietary fiber. Nutritional content of these recipes is based on food composition data in The Pampered Chef database. Variations in ingredients, products and measurements may result in approximate values. Each analysis is based on ingredients initially listed and does not include optional ingredients, garnishes, fat used to grease pans or serving suggestions, unless noted. Recipes requiring milk are based on 2 percent reduced-fat milk. Recipes requiring ground beef are analyzed based on 90 percent lean ground beef. Recipes requiring ground turkey are analyzed based on 93 percent lean ground turkey. Recipes labeled as LIGHT have 30 percent or less calories from fat.

Metric Conversion Chart

Volume Measurements (dry)

⅛ teaspoon = 0.6 mL
¼ teaspoon = 1.25 mL
½ teaspoon = 2.5 mL
¾ teaspoon = 3.75 mL
1 teaspoon = 5 mL
1 tablespoon = 15 mL
2 tablespoons = 30 mL
¼ cup = 50 mL
⅓ cup = 75 mL
½ cup = 125 mL
⅔ cup = 150 mL
¾ cup = 175 mL
1 cup = 250 mL

Recipes in this cookbook have not been tested using metric measures. When converting and preparing recipes with metric measures, some variations in quality may be noticed.

Volume Measurements (fluid)

1 fluid ounce (2 tablespoons) = 30 mL
4 fluid ounces (½ cup) = 125 mL
8 fluid ounces (1 cup) = 250 mL
12 fluid ounces (1½ cups) = 375 mL
16 fluid ounces (2 cups) = 500 mL

Weights (mass)

1 ounce = 30 g
4 ounces = 125 g
8 ounces = 250 g
12 ounces = 350 g
16 ounces = 1 pound = 500 g

Dimensions

⅛ inch = 3 mm
¼ inch = 6 mm
½ inch = 1 cm
¾ inch = 2 cm
1 inch = 2.5 cm

Oven Temperatures

250°F = 120°C
275°F = 140°C
300°F = 150°C
325°F = 160°C
350°F = 180°C
375°F = 190°C
400°F = 200°C
425°F = 220°C
450°F = 230°C